Naperville's Genevieve

A Daughter's Memoir

Caryl Towsley Moy

All net profits from the sale of this book will be donated to the Naperville Heritage Society.

Genevieve Towsley

DEDICATED TO

Genevieve's niece, Rita Harvard

Whose love and care were such that she was thought of as another daughter.

Rita Harvard with Genevieve Christmas 1985

Contents

Acknowledgements xi
Introduction xiii

01 Early Years 1
02 Pioneer Childhood in Idaho 7
03 Additional Idaho Stories 37
04 Transitions 41
05 College Days 45
06 Myron Towsley 49
07 Family Additions 59
08 Wife and Mother 63
09 The Depression 73
10 The Home Front 79
11 Vacations 85
12 The Clarion Years 97
13 Naperville Sun Beginnings 115
14 The Journalist Becomes An Historian 123
15 Inclusion and Diversity 135
16 Genevieve's Favorite Subjects 143
17 Genevieve's Faith and Her Church 159
18 Retirement: A New Beginning 169
19 Honors and Recognitions 187
20 Others' Thoughts 195
21 Her Spirit Lives On 205
22 Friends' and Family Favorites—Genevieve's Recipes 217
    Genevieve's Rolls *219*
    Ice Box Doughnuts *221*
    Buttermilk Waffles *223*
    Egg and Ham Brunch Strata *224*
    French Puffs *225*
    New England Clam Chowder *226*
    Mimi's Ham Loaf Balls *227*
    Sauce *227*
    Beer Braten *228*

Gravy *229*
Sweet Potato Casserole *230*
Genevieve's Pumpkin Pie *231*
Lemon Fluff *232*
Christmas Crescents *234*

ACKNOWLEDGEMENTS

Donna De Falco, experienced writer, admirer of Genevieve, and lover of Naperville history

The Naperville Sun staff, Ted Slowick, Tim West, Diana Kiabi, Kathy Millen, Cheri Zaras

Naperville Heritage Society, Peggy Frank, Executive Director, Bryan Ogg, Research Archivist,

Kim Butler, North Central College Archivist

Mary Lou Cowlishaw, 41st District Representative, Illinois Legislature, 1982-2002

Dr. Michael Ebner, Professor Emeritus, Lake Forest College

Glenna Holloway, widely published writer and poet

Margaret Barnes Yonker, author of Lone Feather and The Settlers

Helen Fraser, author of Footsteps through Old Naperville

James Fancher, First Congregational Church, Naperville, achivist

L. Gay Davidson, Springfield, owner of Computer Help

Mary Rose Martin, Springfield's best English teacher, retired

Barbara Brayton Nelson and Rita Fredenhagen Harvard, Loving nieces

Jennie, Eric, Laurie, and Philip Moy, our helpful sons and their computer savvy wives

My husband, Dick, for his celebrating encouragement and support

INTRODUCTION

I loved and respected my mother, Genevieve Towsley, very much, but why write her biography? Even a few family members were curious when I told them of my intentions. Recently there has been an unusual amount of interest in her life, which has recognized her unique contributions through her writing in the *Naperville Sun* for over 40 years, about Naperville, Illinois, and its history. In 1999 the Century Walk Committee in Naperville chose her as the city's first citizen to be the subject for the sculpture they were placing among other art works commissioned to celebrate Naperville in the 20th century. Life size, cast in bronze, she sits on a bench, notebook in hand, pen poised to write down her impressions to craft her next column for *The Naperville Sun*. In 2006, the Naperville Heritage Society placed her name on the Wall of Honor in the replica Pre-Emption House at Naper Settlement. This distinction was given because it was her writing that influenced many to support the organizing of the society, which saved so many of the city's historic buildings. In 2006, I was approached by several Naperville area media sources that were doing features about her, as part of the 175th anniversary of the town's beginnings. I could tell that many had information gaps as we talked. Also, there are many personal and family stories about her that make her an even more colorful personality than was revealed in her public life. I no longer feel an adolescent embarrassment when she is in the spotlight and I have come to appreciate what a unique role model she has been for me and others.

I am pleased that a lot of people want to know more about this Naperville citizen. What shaped her character? What were her "family scripts," those unstated family truths that are believed and influence the behavior of more than one generation? How did she become the person to make such a difference in what did and what didn't happen in this community? If she hadn't uncovered the fact that a dog racing track was going to be built in Naperville, the town could well have had a very different future. It was her publicizing a small group's concern that the St. John's Episcopal Church was saved and restored. It was the beginning of Naper Settlement, the outstanding prairie village museum.

To those who don't live within the city boundaries of Naperville, why should they care about this little known woman writer who lived in that suburban Chicago community? Genevieve Towsley's story is one that has often been repeated in little towns as well as big cities throughout the nation. As a young girl growing up on the high plains of Idaho, she lived out her father's dream of "going west" from the Chicago suburb of Oak Park. Actually, she was the third generation of a pioneering family because her grandfather came west to Illinois from upstate New York with that same dream. Unfortunately, Genevieve also lived through her parents' disappointments and weathered the storms of the Great Depression and two world wars. In time, her parents' sacrifices and their dreams for their daughter's future led them back to the Chicago area and to Naperville where Genevieve attended college.

These experiences and her education ultimately shaped her with gifts for writing and illuminating for future generations of not only Naperville and DuPage County citizens, but of those elsewhere in Illinois and throughout the country who celebrate the past as they seek to make the future a better place.

My husband, Dick, loves saying his mother-in-law is cast in bronze. Enthusiastic about this project, he encouraged me to work with a more experienced writer. I immediately thought of Donna DeFalco who first introduced herself to me at a Naper Settlement founders' event, saying, "Your mother is my role model. I even use the same kind of pen she used." Further conversation revealed we had more in common than just an admiration for Genevieve. Donna, a professional writer with the Settlement, is an enthusiastic alumna of Sangamon State University, now the University of Illinois at Springfield, where I was a professor for 21 years. It has been a joy to work with her.

Once I began Genevieve's story, I had hoped that I would remember more details. When that didn't happen as I had hoped, I asked Diana Kiabi at *The Naperville Sun* if the computer list of all of Genevieve's articles from 1954 to 1994 was still available. With staff assistance it was found. We planned to get this list while visiting in Naperville in the fall of 2007. We expected this would lead to many long hours reading microfilm at Naperville's Nichols Library. That day Cheri Zaras, receptionist at the front desk at *The Sun*, heard Diana mention the name Genevieve Towsley and asked her to repeat it. She then said, "I saw a big cardboard box with that name on it at the loading dock this morning when I came in. It's probably been there awhile. I just never noticed it before." Nor had anyone else. It contained almost 90% of the articles Genevieve Towsley had written in her half century of writing, even including many from *The Naperville Clarion*! The miraculous appearance of these brown and crumbling pages provided real depth for this story of Naperville's Genevieve.

CARYL TOWSLEY MOY

01
Early Years

The following is based on stories my mother, Genevieve Towsley, told me about her family history and how her parents and siblings reacted to the news of her upcoming birth, which was quite a surprise to everyone!

My grandmother, Clara Brayton, was tending her garden on Cuyler Avenue in Oak Park, Illinois, on a sunny day in August of 1906, thinking about her family. Her two children, Merle and Louise, were doing well. Merle was a strapping teenager. Louise was in her twelfth year and very artistic. Her beloved husband, George Herbert, my grandfather (Grandma called him Bert), had a good job in sales with the Robert Gordon heating firm in Chicago. It was an easy commute for him from Oak Park. Clara was 38. Clara and Bert had lost an infant son, Robert, some 15 years earlier, but by now they both had been able to put that sad day behind them. No longer did Clara fear dying from tuberculosis like her sister Myrtle had. She had been able to travel to New Mexico for sunshine and better care and had fully recovered. Soon Merle would graduate from high school. Clara's mother, Genevieve's grandmother Mary Metzler, lived with the family in the cramped house they rented on Cuyler Avenue. This was mostly manageable despite Mary's occasional paranoid attacks against Bert, and her inclination toward neighborhood gossip.

As Clara stopped to pull weeds, she wondered if she could be experiencing an early menopause. About this time she realized she'd missed several periods. Was it in June or even May since her last one? Then she realized she must be pregnant again. It was nearly 12 years since she had delivered Louise. Bert was as surprised as Clara, but both were delighted with the possibility of another child. Merle and Louise were excited, too. It was a good time for the family to find a house of their own and stop paying rent. Bert located a nearby lot for sale, served as his own contractor, and immediately began overseeing the building of an impressive 10-room home on Harvey Avenue. Clara would have a conservatory for her beloved plants. They moved in just before Genevieve's birth on February 3, 1907. With such a lyrical name as Genevieve, they agreed no middle name was needed.

A 10-room house! This was far more lavish than either Clara or Bert had experienced growing up. Clara's father, Noah Metzler, was a harness and buggy whip maker in New Paris, Indiana before the turn of the century. Both Mary and Noah had grown up on farms in rural Indiana.

Bert's parents, John and Lydia (Palmer) Brayton, had come from upstate New York. They had run a small private school prior to coming West in a covered wagon. They settled briefly in Indiana, then staked a claim near Kankakee,

Genevieve's Birth Place
221 N. Harvey, Oak Park Illinois

Illinois where Bert's father farmed. Bert, his sister Mary, and younger twin brothers were all born there. One of the twins had clubbed feet and was very sickly. Unexpectedly, the healthier twin contracted pneumonia in his first month and died. Because it was winter, the dead infant's body was removed to an unheated part of the house and the family waited, expecting to have a single funeral for both twins. But baby John lived and gathered strength, so after about six weeks, the family gave the dead twin a proper burial. When Bert was about six, his father, John senior, still in his 40s, died suddenly. Lydia, now on her own with three children, returned to Indiana and opened a boarding house in Valparaiso for students at Northern Indiana Normal School and Business Institute. This way she could make a living, and her children could live at home and eventually attend college. Bert and Clara met when Clara was attending that college, which is now Valparaiso University.

Genevieve told about a couple of incidents that reflected her family's happy life at 221 Harvey. Genevieve's older sister, Louise, and her favorite friend, Helen Blaze were bosom pals. One day the phone rang just as the mailman delivered a package. Grandma Clara answered the phone, "No, Louise isn't here. She's gone to Helen Blaze's." Hearing this gentlewoman say these words shocked the postman until Clara explained.

In the postman's daily rounds, which included the Brayton residence, he became acquainted with Bernice, the maid, who worked for the family. When he finally got up his courage to ask her for a date, the young lady agreed to go out with him. Of course, he was out of his postman's uniform when he came to call for her and Clara was surprised when the girl came right back into the kitchen unexpectedly. "He's bald!" she exclaimed. That discovery surprised both women. Obviously, Bernice overcame her surprise since they later married.

For Grandma Clara, the family's lifestyle in Oak Park was pleasant, but Theodore Roosevelt became president in 1901 and greatly influenced the "Go West" movement. In 1902 the Land Reclamation Act was passed encouraging development of irrigation projects in arid and semi-arid regions like southern Idaho. Grandpa heard a distant cousin regale his relatives with tales about property he'd just bought in Idaho. Those stories brought back happy memories of his life on the farm near Kankakee. Bert remembered it as a good life. The only reason his mother had left the farm was because her husband had died, and she had to find a way to support her young family.

In 1909, while in Idaho on business, Grandpa Bert was hooked on the promotions for the "Valley of Eden." He purchased 80 acres. Genevieve's "Childhood in Idaho" story describes this. Although this was Bert's dream, he began to realize that this impulsive decision was a difficult one for Clara. To help her see how she would adapt to this immense change of lifestyle, the family moved for a short time into an apartment with fewer conveniences in Oak Park. Then, in May of 1915, the Brayton family headed west.

02

Pioneer Childhood in Idaho

Through the years, we heard stories about Genevieve's childhood, both from her and from other relatives. She seemed to be a most determined girl who was unusually energetic and very competent. When the John Wayne movie, *True Grit,* came out in 1969, the young girl in that film, Mattie Ross, seemed to personify the family's image of what Genevieve was like at that age in the west. Mother didn't deny that impression.

In 1976, many journalists were writing about their memories in honor of the nation's historic bicentennial. My mother, Genevieve Brayton Towsley, joined them. In late November and early December of 1976, she wrote a vivid three-part series of her experiences as a pioneer child on a ranch near Jerome, Idaho. These recollections made up her "Story of the Week" in three issues of *The Naperville Sun.* In November 1977, the Northern Illinois Newspaper Association announced she had won first place in the

Association's Local Feature Category for this vivid story. We are grateful to *The Naperville Sun* for allowing Genevieve's own story concerning this significant time of her life, 1915-1923, to be included here.

Genevieve Remembers

Accounts of Naperville's early settlers have been my special forte in the years I have been writing my "Skylines" features for the SUN. Now I have the temerity to write my own experiences, since my family, too, were early settlers – not of Naperville, of course, but of Jerome, Idaho.

We Braytons did not trek westward in a Conestoga wagon, as did the Erbs and the Givlers, nor did we ever flee from Indians, as did Clarissa Hobson and her children. The prairies and the plains had been settled, and railroads crisscrossed the land, by the time we joined the host of adventuresome Americans that were lured to take up claims in the sagebrush desert of southern Idaho and other western states. Land developers in that era made just as glowing the potential of irrigated tracts, as do those of today who ballyhoo their projects in the sun country of the southwest.

A dog-eared booklet printed in 1909 and detailing the glory and promise of the development in the Jerome area, has been furnished to me by my nephew, Robert Burks Jr., who was born and resides to this day on the North Side Tract, as the development was called. Here are some samples of the rhetoric employed:

> *"No land was so ably made ready for the husbandman as this North Side Tract in the great valley of the Snake ... Canals, laterals, and waste ditches have wormed their net-work through the*

richest and most fertile of soils, soils enriched by the ages. And through this labyrinth is passed the key that is unlocking Nature's richest gift ... its precious treasure – water. In a few short years, our valley will occupy the most exalted position in the 'Inland Empire.' Our fruits, our cereals, our hogs, our cattle, our dairies, our apiaries will astound the world ... We have studiously avoided threadbare catch phrases and word painting; with what we have back of us we can convince the people who are honestly seeking to better their condition..."

In contrast to the immense ranches that were developed on the dry lands of the plains, those which the North Side Canal Company offered on the North Side Tract, were in 40-acre parcels, with most of the buyers contracting for 80, 120, or 200 acres. Irrigated farming requires intensive care, with the farmer daily "changing the water" – channeling it to different fields and opening the little corrugations in order that every foot of the land is supplied with adequate moisture. Limited acreage is made mandatory, not only by the additional labor required to cultivate an irrigated farm, but also by the original cost charged for "water rights" and the annual fee for water delivered to a farmer's ditches.

Our claim lay five miles southwest of Jerome, one of the four town sites that were established in 1908, when the North Side Canal Company developed the complex irrigation systems which made possible cultivation of 180,000 acres of sagebrush desert. This tract of 280 square miles was situated along the north bank of the Snake River, where it cuts through a canyon 500 feet deep.

Purchasers of the land, which was developed under the Carey Act, paid $35.50 per acre – 50 cents an acre to the government for the land, and $35 to the canal company for the water rights. In order to purchase the government land, the buyer had to "prove up" on it. This entailed erecting a two-room dwelling, six months of residence, and growing a crop on one-eighth of the acreage. These stipulations were placed upon the purchase in order to discourage land speculators.

Before our Idaho venture, our family had been typical of many who lived in Oak Park, Ill., in the early years of this century. Soon after that village began to flourish, Papa and Mamma, the names I always called them, had rented a small house on North Cuyler Avenue. It nicely accommodated them, my brother Merle, my sister Louise, and my grandmother Metzler.

Papa commuted to Chicago's Loop each day on the Lake Street "L," working as a contact man for a heating and ventilating contracting firm. In his spare time, he was involved in the village's politics, working in campaigns to get friends elected. Mamma had her church and club activities to interest her.

Merle was 16 and Louise 11, when Mamma informed the family she was going to have another child. (I was later assured that pleasure was mixed with the family's surprise.) To accommodate their expanding family, a lot was purchased at 221 N. Harvey in the village, and Papa served as his own general contractor for the 10-room house he built there. It was completed, and the family occupied it shortly before my birth, Feb. 3, 1907.

It was in 1909 that Papa, while on a business trip to Boise, Idaho purchased the Idaho property. A cousin of his had bought 200 acres on the North Side Tract "as an investment," and had urged Papa to do likewise. Since I was only two years old, the purchase made no impression upon me, but as I

Idanha Ranch near Jerome, Idaho

grew older, I sensed that Mamma was not enthusiastic about Papa's impulsive investment.

Since Papa was engaged in business, he sent my brother out to "prove up" on the land. Merle was the real pioneer of the family. Within a few months he had a two-room "shack" built in which to live; he had grubbed out the sagebrush on a number of acres; and he had planted a field in alfalfa. Thus all the contingencies of securing our claim had been met.

Papa had contracted for 200 acres, but soon after his purchase, he relinquished 120 acres to a group of his luncheon companions, an action he much regretted later. Day after day he regaled them with the promise of this new land, insisting "with the right amount of water applied at the right time, the desert becomes the Garden of Eden." They formed the Idanha Company, using the Indian word for Idaho. Papa was one of the stockholders in the company, too, and managed that farm as well as ours when we eventually went to Idaho to live.

I do not know whether Papa gave any consideration to the type of soil our land had when he purchased it. It was part of a five-mile strip that bordered the canyon of the Snake and which was almost pure sand. The land that lay farther north had a clay-like consistency that resisted erosion better. Consequently, the farms along the river were planted mostly in alfalfa or pasture, crops that did not require planting and cultivating every spring. The farms away from the river produced bumper crops of wheat or sugar beets.

Papa's memories of his boyhood on a farm in Kankakee County spurred him to encourage my brother to continue developing the farm, since he himself looked forward to it as a refuge from city life. Merle supervised the building of a six-room, two-story house and cleared more acres for cultivation. In the summer of 1910, Mamma and I went to Idaho on the train. Although my brother's need of a housekeeper was my mother's excuse for going, I think she was eager to see the land and the home where she would very likely live some day.

My first childhood memories are associated with that trip. I remember being bitten by a little black-and-tan dog when we stopped en route in Omaha to visit cousins. I remember sleeping in a berth on the train with Mamma and having to wait a long time in a tiny, dingy station when we changed trains for the branch line that ran to Jerome. I remember falling into an irrigation ditch, taking rides in a buggy, and being surprised that we had oil lamps instead of electricity, no telephone, and no bathroom. Water for drinking and cooking was hauled from the well of a neighbor, Bill Zahn. (Only recently I discovered that he was an uncle of Naperville's Norman Zahn.) Mother cooked and baked on a range that she stoked with chunks of sagebrush.

In 1912, my sister, Louise, then 16, went out to spend the summer with my brother. When she returned she announced she was engaged to marry a Virginian, Robert Burks, who, with two brothers, had "proved up" on several hundred acres. Concerned that she had acted too impulsively, my parents persuaded her to wait several years for marriage in order that "Bob" might establish himself better.

Louise's prospect of making a life in Idaho influenced my parents to reach the same decision. Papa built up my enthusiasm for moving to a farm by promising me a horse to ride. I started a bank account for that purpose, and each night would coax Papa to give me any "buffalo nickels" he might have collected that day. Those nickels had only just been minted and were not yet in wide circulation.

Louise and Bob's wedding ceremony was performed in our home in January, 1915. The following May, Papa, Mamma, and I moved west. Papa had contracted for a freight car to transport all our household goods, farm equipment, furnace and radiators for a heating system, and a windmill, pipe, and a huge water tank, in order to provide a water system. To get Mamma's consent and cooperation to forsake her comfortable life style in Oak Park, Papa promised her he would equip our home on the farm with all the modern conveniences she was used to enjoying.

The first project undertaken after arrival in Idaho was drilling a well. The drillers had to go more than 150 feet, mostly through solid rock, before reaching the water level. A three-story "well house" was then erected, and the base of the windmill, as well as the cast-iron storage tank, placed on the third floor. In this manner, a gravity-feed plumbing system was achieved. Ours was one of the few homes on the tract to have running water. The three-story well house became a landmark, since most homesteaders still lived in their two-room dwellings.

In drilling the well a "blow-hole" was encountered. This was a cavity underground, out of which 46-degree air blew. Being a ventilation expert, Papa arranged to pipe this to a compartment on the first floor of the well house, affording us natural refrigeration for all but the hottest weather, when we had to haul 50-pound cakes of ice from Jerome for our ice box.

During the eight years that we lived on the farm, we never had electricity. The mantles of our gasoline lamp gave bright light for reading, but most of our evening's work was done by the light of kerosene lamps and lanterns. Mamma continued to cook on the range, burning sagebrush or coal, but in summer switched to a three-burner kerosene stove with a portable oven.

I gave Papa no peace until I had the horse he had promised. Merle already had a handsome work team – two bays, named Tom and Bess – and a grey riding horse named Dolly. While looking for a horse that would double for driving as well as for riding, Papa accepted the loan of a horse from Louise's husband, Bob. Old Bones was a gentle, 20-year-old race horse that had been "put out to pasture." Bob insisted he would serve my purpose while I was learning to ride.

My first ride was a family event. Old Bones stood docilely while he was bridled, and while Papa tightened the cinch to my new saddle, brought from Chicago, around his belly. Mamma waited anxiously while Papa helped me to mount. Hazel Blakemore our "hired girl" ($2 per week!), had been elected to ride with me on Dolly. Our destination was our mail box, one mile away.

At first we walked our horses, to give me the feel of being astride as I practiced guiding Old Bones by pulling on the reins. Hazel then put Dolly into a trot and Old Bones kept pace. Bumping up and down, I grabbed the saddle horn and tried to hide my discomfort and trepidation. Hazel attempted to teach me to post in order to save me the jar of Old Bones' every stride, but I was too busy just trying to stay on. After reaching the mail box without incident, we turned around and headed home down the sandy road, through the sagebrush.

We had gone perhaps a quarter of a mile, when I heard the footsteps of a horse galloping behind us. As it approached, the rider, a neighbor boy, called out, "You learning to ride, Genevieve?" He attempted to come alongside us, but Old Bones exploded into action, taking off at lightening speed. Once more he was back at the race track, attempting to keep ahead of any horse that would challenge him! I held on tight while Hazel and Russell tried to keep pace, prompting Old Bones to run all the faster. My hat and hair ribbons flew off. The wind whistled past my ears. Glad to see we were almost home, I worried what Old Bones would do when we reached our gate. I soon found out. He slackened pace not at all, and then, as if he knew he had won the race, stopped in his tracks. Only my tight grip on the horn prevented me from flying over his head.

Shaking with fright, when Hazel helped me to dismount, I was soon enjoying the praise of Russell and the family for successfully riding a runaway horse. Hazel and I took daily rides after that, until I mastered mounting, dismounting, controlling my horse, and adjusting to his various paces.

Papa soon purchased a three-year-old black mare that was broken to drive as well as to ride. "Black Beauty," as we named her, was soon shortened to "Beauty." She became the family's link with the outside world – pulling us in our buggy to Jerome to do our weekly shopping, to my sister's cottage, six miles away, to Canyonside church, and to social gatherings. I rode her to friends' homes, to Sunday school and Christian Endeavor society, to 4-H clubs, and to my piano teacher's home. Even after Papa bought our Dort touring car in 1917, Beauty was by no means replaced.

None of the roads were improved, and, even in the best of weather, some were so sandy they were impassable in a car. In winter, Papa put the Dort up on blocks in our machine shed (to protect the tires), and we depended once again on Beauty and the buggy to take us places. She never faltered, although the roads were often clogged with snow drifts, or after a thaw, deep with mud. Our open rig gave no protection from the cold nor from the winds that blew unceasingly across the sagebrush. Long underwear, high-buttoned shoes, woolen petticoats and dresses, and sheep-lined coats were supplemented with scarves, mittens, galoshes, lap robes, and even foot-warmers – flat soap-stones heated on the back of the range. Each trip in winter was like an expedition, since Beauty could navigate the roads no faster than a walk, and nearly two hours would be consumed before we reached Jerome. If we returned after dark, we depended upon her to keep to the road in the darkness.

I remember that first summer as one of excitement and satisfaction, for the most part. There were inconveniences at first, but the well and the heating and plumbing systems were completed before winter closed in. Mother, who had long been an ardent gardener, laid out flower beds in the front yard, planted a large vegetable garden plus raspberry, blackberry, dewberry, gooseberry, currant bushes and strawberry plants. She acquired a flock of chickens and happily gathered the eggs.

One happening that summer marred our pleasure in the new home and way of life. The years before Papa, Mamma, and I arrived, Merle had been operating the farm. After we came, Papa automatically took over its management, making decisions with which Merle would not always agree. Tension developed, and Merle became genuinely hostile when he recognized that his authority was gone and his opinions given no consideration. One day, during a particularly heated argument, Merle threatened to leave. Mamma tried to intercede and reconcile her two men, but failed. Merle stamped upstairs, pulled his trunk out of the closet and packed his belongings. More pleading on Mamma's part was useless, and Papa refused to try to dissuade him. Merle left the house. I cried, and so did Mamma, when a friend came to take him to the train station. He never returned.

SCHOOL DAYS

Getting to school in Idaho was nothing like getting to school in Oak Park. In Oak Park, our home was in the same block as the William Bye School. I could run out our back door and through the school playground to reach the building in two minutes. In Idaho, I rode in a "school wagon" five miles to the school in Jerome.

The developers of the tract had erected a bank and a hotel with ornate Spanish architecture as the nucleus of the town of Jerome. A school district was organized on a centralized plan, bringing elementary pupils in wagons from as far away as eight miles to the grade school built in the town. Several one-room schools were erected to serve those children whose families lived on the outskirts of the irrigated tract.

The wagons were large vehicles, covered with black canvas, and had bench-like seats along the sides to accommodate 16 children. The overflow, children who boarded as we neared the town, stood in the middle until we reached the school. The driver, on a seat in front, separated from us by a canvas curtain, was supposed to control the pupils as well as his team. He was not always successful. There was vying for seats next to special friends. Boys got into arguments and scuffles. The language I heard contributed decidedly to my vocabulary, much to Mamma's and Papa's dismay.

In spring and fall it was daylight when the wagon stopped at our corner to allow me to board, but in winter it was still dark, and by the time I returned, it was dusk. Those two-hour rides, night and morning in the middle of winter, are still a nightmare to me. When the thermometer hovered close to zero, Mamma made me take foot-warmer and lap robe, much to my embarrassment. Still my feet would be blocks of ice at the end of the ride, and the numbness would last until recess. Worse yet were the burning, itching chilblains I suffered, and for which Mamma could find no remedy.

When I entered fourth grade in the fall of 1915, I was a stranger to all but two neighbor boys who rode in my school wagon – Russell Emmett and Waldo Blakemore. Miss Summerville, the teacher, was understanding, however, and I soon made friends. One girl, Thelma Robinson, and I became "chums," a relationship that lasted throughout our stay in Idaho, and contributed immensely to my enjoyment in school. In her home, which was a few doors from the school, I was always welcome, and I spent many "overnights" there. Because I had several unfortunate experiences in which I was bitten by bed-bugs in the homes of friends, Mamma was very cautious in allowing me to accept overnight invitations. At the Robinson home, however, that hazard did not exist. I have always wondered why so many Idaho homes were infested with bed-bugs, even with homemakers who had high standards of housekeeping.

I rode the school wagon while attending fourth, fifth and sixth grades. In the winter of 1918, our neighbors held a meeting to discuss organizing a one-room school for our community. They voted in favor of it, deciding to name it Lucerne (Alfalfa) Valley School. An older lady, Mrs. Pogue, was hired as the teacher. She and her husband lived in the two-room shack which Merle had originally built in proving up on our farm. The school and its two outhouses were built across the road in the middle of the sagebrush, where no one had staked a claim.

Russell, Waldo and I made up the seventh grade,

the highest grade in the school. Altogether, we were probably 20 pupils. Under Mrs. Pogue's competent and motherly instruction, we seemed like a big family. At recess and at noon there were group games for all – Pom Pom Pullaway, Cheeze-it, Red Light, Anti-I-Over and others. My education surely did not suffer that year, and I remember it as one of my most pleasant school years.

Because the decision had been made that eighth-graders should all attend the school in town, and because there were not enough students to fill a school wagon, we were transported in an Overland touring car. Although Mrs. Prentiss, our eighth-grade teacher, had rather a forbidding personality, she was an extraordinary teacher, especially thorough when it came to grammar and sentence structure. No one passed from her grade without knowing all about subjects, predicates and the uses of the different parts of speech.

Jerome's one school accommodated high school classes in four rooms on the top floor until 1920, when a high school was built on a square block reserved for that purpose. Everyone adjusted to the crowded conditions when I was freshman, but we appreciated the new facility all the more when it was completed.

Although the school board had, from the beginning, provided transportation for elementary pupils, no arrangements were made to get the high school students who lived in the country into town. Most of us who continued beyond eighth grade rode horseback.

Faced with the prospect of riding the five miles to school and back each day, I asked Papa to get me another riding horse. Beauty had served well when I was an inexperienced rider, but she was primarily a driving horse. She was large boned, had a rather lumbering gait, and never developed any speed. Papa agreed that I deserved a better horse, and once again he turned to Bob to help us obtain one. He produced Spider, a steel-grey mare that was gentle but very high strung. Bob held her when I first tried to mount her since she refused to stand. Once I was in the saddle, she took off, literally flying out our driveway. She sped down the road, giving me the smoothest ride I ever had had. I let her run for a mile, and then reined her in, using all the strength I could muster. We turned around, and she would have run all the way home, had I not kept a tight rein on her. I knew I had a superb riding horse.

Those rides were the best part of the school day. Along the way, other riders joined us until, as we neared Jerome, we became quite a cavalry. Riding abreast, except when we encountered a horse-drawn vehicle or an occasional car, we argued who had the best horse, or discussed our teachers and school activities. Sometimes we ran races, and Spider usually led them all.

Once we arrived at the school, we hitched our horses in the barn, which was provided. Because it was never, to my knowledge, cleaned out from the beginning of the school year to the end, I tried to be among the first to get to the barn in order to pick one of the cleaner stalls. With other girl riders I headed for the girls' restroom to remove our full riding bloomers that we wore under our dresses. No doubt the pungent odor of the horse barn still clung to our shoes and clothing when we went to classes, but it was common to many of us, and our peers did not deny us acceptance.

When winter closed in, I gave up horseback riding in favor of finding lodgings in Jerome, within walking distance of school. I would stay in town during the week, but on Friday after school, Papa or Mamma would drive in with Beauty to take me home for the weekend, driving me back on Sunday afternoon. A generous supply of Mamma's baked and canned goods, home-cured ham, butter, cottage cheese, and eggs would go with me. My most enjoyable winter was spent with family friends – a young couple with a baby.

Other winters, two sisters, also students, and I rented one large room in a store building. The landlady, a chiropractor, had her office and living quarters in an adjoining unit in the building. Our room was sparsely furnished, and our only light at night was that given by two 40-watt bulbs dangling from wires from the ceiling.

In order not to strain our eyes while studying, we bought 100-watt bulbs and replaced the lesser ones. My cot was under one of the lights. A noise in the middle of one night awakened me, and I roused up to see by the light coming in from the lamp post on the street, our landlady with a butcher knife in one hand, standing over me. She was snatching the light bulb. Afraid she would attack me if I screamed, I lay quietly until she went back into her room. My roommates had seen her, too, and for the remainder of the night we did not sleep.

We moved out the next day. I stayed temporarily with friends and then moved into a vacant room behind a confectionery store. My folks supplied me with a cot, table, chair, and a one-burner oil stove. I had little time to be lonely, since I was a member of the high school glee club, and we were rehearsing "The Mikado," the school's first musical, every night. The fact that I had the role of Katisha shows how desperate they were for soloists. I also was writing "personals" for the Jerome County Journal, my first journalistic effort. I received five cents a column-inch.

Farm children all had chores to do, and I was no exception. Papa would never have suggested Mamma or I should milk the cows or work the fields, as some of our friends did, but we had plenty of work, just the same. After our first summer, when there was no longer money for a hired girl, dishwashing became my job. Dishes weren't so bad, but how I hated the pans – especially if Mamma had put them directly over the fire to hasten her cooking. That soot! Ugh! After several years when Papa developed a small dairy herd, we acquired a cream separator. Cream was separated from the milk by centrifugal force pulsing through 30 little metal leaves that fitted tightly together. There was always a residue that clung to each leaf, which had to be washed one by one. It was tedious and smelly. Churning butter every week was another chore I found tiresome.

Most of the berry picking was assigned to me – a job I enjoyed, except for gooseberries, blackberries and dew berries. They had "prickers." Our small orchard yielded beautiful fruit those seasons when the frost did not kill the blossoms. I picked cherries, apricots and plums by the peck for canning and preserving. Of course, I helped with hulling strawberries and pitting cherries. Mother canned vegetables, fruits and even meats to last us through the winter.

Feeding the poultry – chickens, turkeys and ducks – and gathering eggs were tasks I enjoyed, and by the time I was a teenager, I begged Papa to let me drive the "derrick team" when a crew of neighbors came to help make hay. It was an easy job. When a load of hay was brought in from the field, a "slip rope" was fastened around it and attached to a pulley and cable. When I drove the derrick team a short distance, it pulled the bundle of hay high in the air by means of a derrick to which the cable ran. The bundle was then guided over to a hay stack by a worker holding

Genevieve, age 14 with her sheep flock

a long rope. He gave it a jerk then, to trip the slip rope and allow the hay to fall on the stack.

Papa soon discovered that operating an irrigated farm meant 12-to14-hour work days. Even though he hired a man to take Merle's place, he rarely found time to mow our large lawn. This distressed Mamma, who had laid out beautiful flower beds in the corners of the lawn. A neighbor suggested we buy several lambs and let them graze on the lawn. After fencing the yard and also the flower beds, Papa bought 10 lambs. One that was black became my special pet, Gretchen by name.

Not only did the lambs solve our mowing problem, they were the start of a flock that increased annually and eventually became one of the main sources of the family's income. Each year the ewe lambs were retained for breeding purposes, while the wethers were sent to market. Since sheep frequently have twins, the flock multiplied rapidly, and Papa hired neighbor boys to herd them each summer in the sagebrush that adjoined our farm. By the time I was 14, I begged for the job, and he was glad to let me do it.

On horseback, and with the help of our shepherd dog, Laddie, I drove the flock of over 100 sheep and lambs out into the brush each morning. Often they grazed close to home, but if the grass had been consumed there, I drove them up the side of the butte which covered the mile section next to our house. At the foot of the butte, an irrigation canal ran, and its banks were lush with sweet clover, which the sheep ate voraciously. If we were close to home, I drove the flock into the barnyard for a siesta during the noon hour while I ate lunch, or I kept them out all day and ate a sack lunch.

I always took a book with me, and during those weeks, through the summers, read all the "Elsie

Dinsmore" and the "Little Colonel" series, as well as the novels by Gene Stratton Porter, Eleanor Porter, Zane Grey, and Grace Livingston Hill Lutz. Sometimes I went swimming in the canal. Occasionally, Laddie would chase and kill jack rabbits. He always brought them to me, and if one was a young one, I skinned it and took it home for a treat for the family's supper.

Those were happy, carefree days.

Family Vacations and Holidays

My memories of the eight years my family lived in southern Idaho are largely of happy times. Not that there were no hard times. Although my parents had reverses that eventually cost them the farm, they rarely expressed their disappointments or anxieties in my presence. Also, with the passing years, I undoubtedly have tended to become nostalgic, and have idealized my childhood.

The six miles that separated us from my sister's family did not prevent us from getting together frequently. Louise's and Bob's three children came singly or together by "grandma's house" for weeklong visits. Babysitting with them was one of my favorite pastimes. If my services were needed at their house on weekends, I rode Beauty or Spider there, but if I went on a school night, I hitched a ride in the school wagon that passed their house.

Our two families took our vacations together. They were camping trips, since we could afford no other kind; and the Sawtooth Mountains, where we usually went, had no overnight accommodations. We could see their peaks, 100 miles distant, from the third-story windows of our well house. In our Dort, and in the Burks' Ford we could, with luck, reach Ketchum (now the site of Sun Valley) in one day.

Beyond our North Side Tract, we drove through desert that included long stretches of lava beds. For our noontime picnic lunch, we aimed to reach The Cottonwoods, a little oasis on the banks of the Wood River in the middle of sagebrush desert. We rarely made that first day's run without getting a puncture or two, traveling over the unimproved, rutted road. Our campsites were in pine woods along fast-running streams. Wading and casting, Bob never failed to bring us a mess of mountain trout for our suppers.

In the summer of 1917, when the Dort was still new and the Burks' first child, Virginia, was only a toddler, our two families drove to Yellowstone Park. I remember Papa's concern, as we drove a stretch of 50 miles of badlands, with our radiator boiling...and again, when the Dort's undercarriage was scraping the center of a deeply rutted road between Howe and Arco. Trucks carrying lead ore had made it impassable for cars, and for 30 miles, Papa had to thread his way through the sagebrush at the side of the road.

Even at age 10, I marveled at the beauty of Yellowstone's waterfalls and geysers, but I best remember how the bears cleaned us out of all the provisions the first night we camped in the park. They left a few onions and a bag of salt, but they broke our jars of canned goods and devoured the ham, bacon, bread, cookies, sugar and lard that Mamma and Louise had provided. We cut our stay short, when we discovered that bread, ordinarily eight cents a loaf, was 50 cents in the park's commissary and all other groceries priced accordingly!

Holidays were family times, too. Two Christmases were especially memorable. Snow had drifted the roads shut, one December 24, when we planned to drive to the Burks' home. Papa declared that the trip was out of the question. I cried. He capitulated. We bundled in our warmest clothes, and they placed me on a stool behind the buggy's seat, shrouded blankets over me, and put a foot warmer at my feet. In the open rig, Mamma and Papa were exposed to the biting winds, but as I huddled in my blanket-tent and as Beauty strained to pull us through the drifts, I heard no complaining. We stopped briefly, while Papa asked our good neighbor, Mr. Blakemore, to do his chores, but the remainder of the trip seemed endless. However, the joyous welcome we received from the Burks made all the efforts worthwhile.

The other unforgettable Christmas was the most meager of the scores I have celebrated, yet none has been more meaningful. I was only 11, but I had begun to notice how carefully Mamma calculated every cent she spent. Without grumbling, she restored to all sorts of creative austerity measures. She traded eggs and butter with the grocer for the few staples which we needed to supplement our own vegetables, fruits, meats and dairy products. The previous summer, she earned "pin money" by taking fresh sweet corn, red raspberries, and other garden produce to town and selling it to a boarding house operator. Hinting to aunts and cousins back in Chicago that she would gladly accept their discarded dresses or coats, she made me outfits from the garments they sent.

Even at Christmastime she was not daunted, infecting Papa and me with her spirit. To take the place of our usual Christmas tree, she suggested that a sagebrush tree would be quite appropriate, and that I should search out a shapely one in the land on each side of our farm that had not as yet been claimed. I meandered through the brush on a snowy day, carefully assessing each bush which was taller than I. Finally choosing one that was full at the bottom and tapering at the top, "like a Christmas tree," I mentally marked its location in relation to our well house, which I could see over the bush tops.

Later, I took Papa with me, and he chopped down the "tree" I had selected. With our German Christmas ornaments and tinsel, and with strings of popcorn, that tree, to my eyes was truly beautiful.

We were not the only farm family experiencing hardship. Mamma was especially concerned for the Blakemores, who lived in a two-room shack covered with tar paper. She suggested we pack a box of gifts for them, and together we went shopping. We chose ten-cent gifts for all of the six children but Althea – the seven-year-old who had walked only with the aid of braces and crutches, since she had had "infantile paralysis." We bought her a doll.

There was a box of Mamma's homemade candy for Mrs. Blackmore and two of Papa's big Delicious apples for Mr. Blakemore. To play Santa Claus, I wore my red bathrobe and hood, when Mamma and I drove with the gifts on Christmas Eve. I quietly placed them by their door, rang the string of bells I carried, and then ran back toward the buggy. As I stumbled into a snow-filled irrigation ditch, I saw the Blakemores' door open and heard Mr. Blakemore exclaim, "Well, I declare! It looks like Santa Claus has been here!" Never have I felt such great Christmas joy!

Except for the one toy I had chosen from a Sears catalog – a doll's bath set – all the gifts under our tree that year were produced by loving hands or our farms. Louise made me new doll clothes for my precious Gretchen; Mamma made me a new dress and Papa a night shirt from material she had on hand. For Louise, there were cans of Mamma's fruit and chicken, and for Bob a live rooster. Papa had built a stand for Mamma's big fern. After watching little Virginia's delight in opening her gifts, and singing "Silent Night" together, we all agreed it had been "a truly special Christmas."

Church and Entertainment

By the time we made our home in the Jerome area, several churches had been established. A young Welshman, Robert Lloyd Roberts, ministered to a Presbyterian congregation in Jerome for several successive summers while he was still a seminary student. He preached Sunday morning in the Jerome church, Sunday afternoon in the Canyonside School, and Sunday evening in a tiny church in the Arcadia neighborhood. We were among the two dozen regular attendants at Canyonside. No matter that our pews were the school desks; we received inspiration from the ardent young preacher. Upon graduating from seminary and getting a call to serve the three parishes full time, he married and brought his bride to live in Jerome.

Since our home was halfway between Canyonside and Arcadia, Mamma invited "Reverend Roberts" to have Sunday supper with us, whenever he had no other obligations. He came often, and we developed a close relationship with him that had an impact on my entire life. His sermons were probably not great, but his living, as well as voicing his Christian faith, was genuinely appealing. By the time I was 13, I was teaching the children's Sunday school class, picking up some of my pupils on the three-mile drive to Canyonside.

The state conference, or camp meeting, was a high point for me. Held in the foothills of the Sawtooths, it had dynamic preachers on the rostrum, among them Dr. John Timothy Stone. I was among the several young people who took his evangelistic message so to heart that we declared our desires to become full-time Christian workers, and signed cards to that effect. Mamma and Papa were not pleased when I told them my decision upon my return home.

I continued the piano lessons I had started in Oak Park, but my resistance to practicing led Mamma to decide that 50 cents a lesson might be put to better use, and thus my musical career ended at age 12. A more interesting and lasting activity was the 4-H Club. Only two projects were offered to girls – canning and baking. I enrolled in both, vying with girls in all the clubs for prizes at the Jerome County Fair. A blue ribbon brought us $1, and a red one, 50 cents. I won $15 one year with my canned fruits and vegetables, and when the jars were sent to the state fair in Boise, I won an additional $4.

Each team of two girls who gave the best demonstration of canning or baking won a trip to the state fair. A friend and I were awarded this privilege, with our demonstration of making baking powder biscuits. It was a doubtful honor, however, since we were the only team in the baking category that competed.

Once a year we enjoyed a week of concentrated culture, when the Chautauqua came to Jerome. Mamma always managed to buy season tickets, and each afternoon, for six days, she and I drove to Jerome, attended a lecture in the afternoon, ate our picnic supper in the park beside the big Chautauqua tent, and joined the spectators in the evening for a play or a concert. In one all-girl orchestra we discovered the Lewis sisters playing violin and cello. They had been Louise's childhood friends in Oak Park. What a pleasant surprise and reunion we had!

I remember fondly my visits to my teenage friends' homes. We discussed the novels we were reading, while we embroidered pillow cases or towels for our hope chests. (Whatever happened to hope chests?)

There were no Cokes or snacks for refreshments. Instead we had homemade cookies and lemonade or cocoa. Country dances, held in homes, met our boy-girl needs, since most of us were "too young to date" according to our parents.

GOING BACK TO CHICAGO

Few of Papa's farming ventures met with success. Familiar with hog raising in his boyhood in downstate Illinois, he invested in some sows, and started a similar operation on our farm. When he realized the land on our tract was not suited to corn production, and the price of feed imported from the Midwest ate up his profit, he disposed of his hogs.

In the bottomland of the canyon of the Snake River, I.B. Perrine each year had a bountiful harvest of fruit from the large orchards he had planted there. His Blue Lakes Ranch was a showplace for all prospective land buyers, and Papa had been impressed. Describing the abundant fruit yield to his associates who had invested in the 120 acres he had shared with them, they were eager to have their land planted to fruit trees. Merle, accordingly, had young Jonathan and Delicious apple trees planted on the entire acreage.

By 1915, when our family arrived, the trees had not yet begun to bear fruit. Between the trees, red clover or potatoes were planted, but the crops were difficult to cultivate and harvest, and the yield was scanty. Even those springs, when the trees burst into spectacular bloom, killing frosts prevented fruit from maturing. Papa had failed to consider that the high cliffs on either side of the canyon, where Perrine had his orchards, had sheltered his trees from the frosts. Finally convinced that fruit production was not feasible, Papa reluctantly and sadly had the whole orchard uprooted and the acreage planted in alfalfa -- the dependable crop that grew in most of our other fields.

Not all our reverses were due to Papa's lack of judgment. Since the Snake had its source in Jackson Lake in the Teton Mountains, when the snowfall there was below normal, our supply of irrigation water ran short the following summer. Ditch riders were forced to reduce the measure of flow in each farmer's main ditch. By August, the canals were sometimes dry, and we got no third cutting of our alfalfa for hay. Prices for the farmers' products were low, and government subsidies had not even been conceived. Freight rates to distant markets ate up any profit that might be realized. I remember a year, when I helped harvest the potato crop, the price was so low that Papa kept them to feed the several hogs we fattened for our own butchering.

In retrospect, I realize how disillusioned Papa was with his farming venture. Instead of living the life of a county squire, as he had supposed, he had to put in 12-14-hour days at real dirt farming. Merle's departure was the first crack in his shattered dream.

Mamma and I had kept in touch with Merle after he returned to Chicago. The heating firm that Papa had long been associated with gave him a position. His joining the National Guard, "in order to ride horseback," led to his being sent to Texas with the Illinois unit to defend our Mexican border against Pancho Villa in 1916. That military experience enabled him to qualify for officers' training and get a commission during World War I with the 23rd Engineers. He served in France, married a French girl, and returned in 1919 with his bride and the rank of captain. When she later came to Jerome to meet his family, the rift between Merle and Papa was permanently mended.

Papa's financial reserves dwindled rapidly. Hired help became more costly, and during the war, men were not even available. High school boys were imported from Chicago to "help the war effort," and one lived with us during the summer of 1918.

A promoter or PR man by inclination and experience, Papa began to despise the drudgery of farm work. Devoted, above all, to his family, he cherished his evenings with Mamma and me, and refused to let his farm chores deprive him of these, which are pleasant memories for me today ... Papa lying on the couch smoking his pipe, Mamma or I reading aloud from a magazine or a book. When Mamma and I would go up to bed, Papa went out to spend the next two hours milking, by hand, our little herd of Guernsey cows. Declaring that as long as he did his milking at twelve-hour intervals, it mattered not to the cows whether he milked them at 6:00 or at 10:00, he acquired a reputation for keeping peculiar hours for a farmer.

His chief concern was for improving life for all the farmers, even if it meant neglecting the demands of his own operation. His first project was getting a group to support a telephone line for our neighborhood. He called a meeting, negotiated with a telephone company, and went to each farmer's door to solicit subscribers. He worked to get the Farm Bureau established in Jerome County, but the venture that proved most beneficial was helping to organize a cooperative creamery. This opened the dairy industry to farmers throughout the tract. They became dairymen, selling their cream to the creamery to be made into Pride of Idaho butter. Mamma and I no longer had to churn butter. The creamery, greatly expanded today, is noted for the superior cheddar cheese made there. It has joined the western chain of Challenge creameries, and Robert Burks Jr. has served on its board of directors.

Papa's activities extended into politics, too. A few aggressive farmers throughout Idaho were seeking to organize. To gain governmental consideration, they joined forces with the newly-organized labor unions, and established the Farmer-Labor party. By 1922, the party had gained sufficient momentum and support to hold a convention for the purpose of nominating a slate of state officers. Mamma and I went with Papa to the convention, held in the state capital at Boise. They chose him to run for Secretary of State. I was very nervous, but proud, too, when he made his acceptance speech.

Campaigning around the irrigated tracts of southern Idaho, he talked to farmers' groups, emphasizing the need for organized efforts to get legislation for their needs. His Republican opponent won the election, but Papa had the satisfaction of getting more votes than the Democratic candidate who was a Rhodes Scholar.

The Brayton family's financial situation became increasingly critical every year following the Armistice. While cream checks paid our basic monthly expenses, sale of our spring lambs and wool did not bring in enough cash to pay taxes, the coal bill for our furnace, the canal company's annual assessment for our water, and extra feed for the livestock. The farm was mortgaged. Once those interest payments were added to other obligations, Papa not only was forced to admit defeat, but also vocalized his distaste for farm work.

What to do? We held a family council with Louise and Bob. To save the farm, it was decided that their family would occupy our house, and Bob would operate our farm on a 50-50 share-crop basis. Papa, Mamma and I would return to Chicago where, at age 57, he hoped he would find employment with a heating firm again.

The departure was hard, especially on Mamma, who had to leave behind most of her cherished things. How sad it was to say good-bye to Louise and her little ones! Papa left first, and accepted the hospitality of Merle and his wife, until he was hired by Robert Gordon, Inc., the firm that Merle had joined when he returned from World War I. Mamma and I waited to move until I completed my junior year at Jerome High School in the spring of 1923.

We rented an apartment in Oak Park where I was graduated from high school. With no family funds to finance a college education for me, I had discarded that ambition; but Papa found a way. He said, "If you select a college in a town close enough to Chicago for me to commute to work, we will move there, and you can live at home while going to school. Somehow we'll manage to pay your tuition."

I chose North Western College (now North Central) in Naperville, a serendipitous decision that I have never regretted.

❋ 03 ❋
Additional Idaho Stories

Although her family struggled financially, Genevieve had fond memories of the years on the Idaho ranch. The difficulty of life in Idaho is revealed in a January 1918 letter that Clara wrote to her relatives in Oak Park.

> *If any of you folks have long gloves that the fingers are worn, I wish you would pass them this way. You see I'm already beginning to plan for my garden next spring. With my short sleeved house dresses, I need long gloves when I work in the garden, and if you ever discard any wool dresses anymore remember I can make them over nicely for Genevieve. I'm wearing the same dresses I brought out, haven't bought a single new dud, except housedresses, and they seem to wear out awfully fast. I made Genevieve a new coat this winter out of*

Louise's old one, and made her a velvet tam out of one of my old hats.

Bert tried to sell our car this fall but I guess it's a good thing he didn't. An auto seems to be a necessity on a farm and I'm sure we wouldn't get another if he sold this one since steel has gone out of sight.

Genevieve's 4H cooking and baking experiences took her to the Idaho State Fair. There, she and her 4H club girl friends were befriended by the head cook for the state Department of Agriculture events at the fair. One evening when he knew he was going to have to prepare a banquet for the governor and other dignitaries, the chef asked the girls if they would help serve. He promised them a dollar each if they would help out. Serving that meal proved to be one of the most embarrassing moments of Genevieve's life. Evidently there was an anteroom, like a butler's pantry, between the kitchen and the dining hall. Dishes were scraped into garbage cans in that room on their way to be washed. As luck would have it, with both her hands carrying filled plates for the guests, Genevieve happened to kick over one of the garbage containers, sending it through the swinging doors and right into the dining hall, dumping smelly food scrapings right under the governor's chair. She was mortified. The head chef told her to keep going, as he quickly attempted to clean up the mess.

The home processing of milk from the family's small herd of cows provided mixed memories for Genevieve. She wrote of how she hated washing the cream separator. One of the products of that process was skim milk, which Grandma thought so unfit for human consumption that it was fed to the pigs. For the rest of her life, Genevieve couldn't make herself drink skim milk, no matter how healthy it was touted to be.

Although Genevieve also hated churning butter as a girl, she always loved fresh butter! Margarine would not be served as a spread on Genevieve's table until butter was relatively scarce and expensive during World War II. While usually a very economical cook, if a recipe called for butter, Genevieve never used a substitute. For her, real butter had a unique flavor that couldn't be duplicated.

Genevieve once confided how she learned about sexuality during those Idaho years. She explained that if she asked Grandma Clara a question about sex, Clara told Genevieve to get the book <u>What Every Young Girl Should Know</u> from the library. This early 1900s "sex education" book was not particularly informative, however. It directed young readers, if the subject of sex came up, to say, "I would rather you would not tell me about it. I will ask my mother . . . Mother tells me everything that I ought to know and she tells me in such a way that makes it very sweet to me, and so I have my little secrets with Mother, and not with other girls."

Genevieve also remembered seeing the word "adultery" in the Ten Commandments. She asked her mother what it meant. Her mother answered sharply, "Don't ask me about that!" As with many young people, Genevieve's mother told her not to ask questions about sex and to get the answer in a book. The book, in turn, told her to ask her mother for the same information. Genevieve probably learned more about sexuality growing up around farm animals than she was able to learn from her mother.

Genevieve loved herding sheep on the Idaho ranch. Her father originally bought several sheep so he wouldn't have to mow the lawn. They developed into a herd of over 100 head. Of course, when the family left Idaho, they left the sheep behind as well. But even years later, whenever we saw sheep from the road as our family traveled about, Genevieve would look at them longingly and repeat in a childlike voice, "sheepies! sheepies!" Knowing of her fondness for sheep, her family and friends would often give her sheep figurines, sheep stuffed toys, sweaters picturing sheep, sheep table decorations, or sheep jewelry.. After many years of "sheep-themed" gifts, her husband Myron finally said, "I wish they wouldn't do that." What bothered him about the sheep knick knacks remained a mystery, but she received a lot fewer sheep gifts after he spoke up.

The Brayton family returned from Idaho in 1923 in time for Genevieve to attend her senior year at Oak Park-River Forest High School. She spoke very little about that year in Oak Park before the family moved to Naperville. I remember only one story she told. It was early in the 1920s when buying, selling and serving alcohol was illegal anywhere in the United States. One warm evening she was visiting a friend while the nextdoor neighbors were having a party on their porch. It was obvious to the girls it wasn't a "dry" party. After a while the party moved inside and, being good, law-abiding Christians, the girls sneaked next door and dumped the neighbors' liquor over the porch railing, feeling quite justified with their actions. When Genevieve recounted this in her mature years, she was embarrassed at her own audacity as a teenager.

/ 04 }

Transitions

In 1924, Grandma Clara packed up her household for another move, this time to Naperville, about 25 miles west of Oak Park, so that her daughter Genevieve could live at home and go to college. This move wasn't as emotionally difficult as the previous two, but there was still fallout from the past.

When the Brayton family left Idaho, it was arranged that Bob Burks, Louise's husband, would continue running the farm and harvesting the crops. This arrangement was short-lived because within a few years the Burks name was all over the southern Idaho papers. Bob learned that Louise had been having an affair with the local superintendent of schools. The superintendent tried to shoot Bob, unsuccessfully. The school administrator then turned the gun on himself and committed suicide. This scandal ended the family agreement for Burks to manage the Brayton farm property, putting a further dent in the Brayton finances.

By 1930, Louise and Bob were divorced. Louise moved back to Illinois with two of her children, Virginia, the oldest, and Brayton, the youngest son. Older son Bobby stayed with his father in Idaho. Louise was able to get a job as a window decorator in one of the Chicago State Street department stores. Clara and Bert worried a bit less until Louise told them she was pregnant. They suspected the father to be the school superintendent.

In desperation and with some guilt, my grandfather Bert approached the family physician. Was there any way an abortion could be arranged? He was told, "There's a doctor in Plainfield who might be able to help." Louise had the abortion and tried to go on managing her life as a divorced mother. This abortion was kept secret until nearly 50 years later when Mother shared this story with me as I was writing our family history for my graduate school project.

Genevieve was aware that her parents always attributed the loss of the farm to this breakup in family tranquility. Because she wanted this family crisis saved "for the record," she made a copy of a letter she had written to her nephew, Robert Burks, in Idaho. He had served on the Northside Canal Board for many years, the same board his grandfather, Bert, had served on in the early 1920s. In 1994, she wrote to Robert, thanking him for sending an old clipping from the Jerome paper.

Thank you for your note and the 1928 clipping. I was aware of most of the contents of the article.

Your mother brought a lot of grief to my parents, your grandparents. Your parents moved into our house in 1923 and your father operated our farm, as well as our land further north. When your parents separated and moved off the farm, Dad couldn't pay taxes on the Idaho farm, nor the cost of water for irrigation so he went through bankruptcy. We eventually lost our Idaho farm.....

Congratulations on your long years of service on the Northside Canal Board. It's hard to realize you are 75....

    Stay well,
       Love, Genevieve

    Genevieve's brother, Merle, had a good experience in the cavalry in the Illinois National Guard in Texas where he guarded the border in Brownsville. He was proud of the horse he was given to ride, and he thought of it as his best friend. While in the guard he changed his name from Merle to William. Musically inclined, he took his violin with him to Texas and started company orchestras wherever he went. Because of his excellent service in the guard, he was recruited into the US 23rd Army's Engineers and sent to France in 1919 to rebuild the war-torn nation. While there, he met and eventually married a woman named France and brought her home to the United States. When he took her to meet his parents, the rift between him and his father was finally repaired. However, it wasn't long before there was one between France and Merle. While Merle was at work, France was having an affair with a stableman on the Hertz farm where she would go horseback riding. That marriage ended, and by 1930 Merle had courted and married Martha Luft.

Caryl Towsley Moy

05
College Days

Genevieve enrolled at North Western College, now North Central College, in Naperville for the fall semester of 1924. Her father, Bert, had been rehired by Robert Gordon and Company and rode the Chicago, Burlington and Quincy Railroad to work in Chicago. The family rented a pleasant frame home on the northwest corner of Jefferson and Eagle streets. Of course, Clara planted a flower garden. A couple of rooms were rented to other women students to supplement the family income. These young women became some of Genevieve's dearest lifelong friends. I called them "Aunt Rose", "Aunt Ethel", "Aunt Peggy", etc.

One Sunday afternoon, two of the girls, Rose and Peggy, urged Genevieve to "bob" her hair. She loved this idea—in fact, it was probably her idea—but one she never could have convinced her mother to allow. She had worn her hair in braids as long as she could remember. Within an hour the transformation was complete. When Clara saw it, she wept profusely. This was the first time Genevieve could remember doing something of which her mother didn't approve. In her later years, whenever Genevieve rode past the Jefferson Street house she would comment, with great nostalgia, about her life there. She had such vivid memories.

Genevieve thrived in college. Her favorite classes were speech and English with professors Guy Oliver and Harold White. By her senior year, she was assisting in both of their classes. Her French teacher, Annette Sicre, became a good friend. She joined the oratory club, entered speech contests and won prizes, thanks to her verbal skills. She also dated a little. One gentleman she dated was Ralph Moy, a farm boy from Mondovi, Wisconsin. She had almost forgotten those couple of dates until years later when I started dating my husband, Dick Moy, who is Ralph's nephew. It's always been fun for me to picture my mother going out with my husband's favorite uncle.

Grandpa Bert even managed to find the funds to buy Genevieve a car. Its engine had to be cranked to get it started and Genevieve didn't have the arm strength to crank it herself, but her friend, Rose Gunther, did. Genevieve quickly learned to always take Rose along for the ride whenever she went driving in her "Rosebud."

When she graduated in June 1928, Genevieve was the only one listed in the North Central's commencement program as graduating with high honors. She had traveled with the college debate team and won second place in the Illinois Intercollegiate Oratorical Contest and second place in oratory at the Pi Kappa Delta convention at Heidelberg College in Tiffin, Ohio. Her entry was printed in the 1928 issue of the college yearbook, <u>The Spectrum</u>.

At that time, air travel was in its infancy; Captain Byrd, a pioneering aviator, had to make a forced landing in the surf and Charles Lindbergh's famous transatlantic flight had occurred just the year before. Inspired by these events, Genevieve used the metaphor of flight, its risks—dense fog, low fuel reserve and faulty compass -- in her prize winning speech. These are her last lines:

> *Unless our youth is equipped with the ability to right its compass, it will lose its sense of direction. It must be trained to adjust its compass to meet emergencies before starting on the great adventure of life.*
>
> *From only one source can the youth of today secure this training—from the youth of yesterday. The youth of yesterday embarked upon a similar adventure not many decades ago. Although they may not have flown so high nor so far, yet there were times when they too encountered fogs and had to conserve their fuel supply. They are the transition between the sham and hypocrisy of yesterday and the frankness and square shooting of today. Better than anyone else can, they can equip youth with knowledge of how to adjust its compass. But oh how cautiously must this knowledge be imparted! For the youth of today is very self sufficient. He invites no admonition or exhortation from his elders—in fact he resents dictation. He wants to find out for himself whether the paint sign on life is genuine. He will take the word of no*

one for all of the intoxicating possibilities that the world has to offer him. Only through a shared life will the youth of today absorb the deepest faiths of the youth of yesterday. Out of the tumult and discipline of family life will the youth of today glean the best. Through constant human contact will the social attitudes and sense of values be acquired. The youth of today is unconscious of receiving, but the youth of yesterday is ever conscious of its giving. The youth of yesterday gets no vacation in this task. It is ever equipping the youth of today with the ability to adjust its compass in time of emergency. Possessing this knowledge the youth of today can fly on to a glorious victory. But if the youth of yesterday fails, the modern youth will fly on to certain disaster—in a dense fog, with low reserve and a faulty compass.

In 1927, the year before Genevieve graduated, North Western College changed its name to "North Central" because name confusion had developed with Northwestern University in Evanston, Illinois, about 50 miles northeast of Naperville. One unwary lad had actually enrolled in the college in Naperville believing he was a student at Northwestern University. Students had a voice in the name change. "Naperville College" didn't sound right and besides it didn't fit the rhythm in the alma mater song, so the name became North Central College. Thus, the North Central alma mater can still be sung with the same enthusiasm.

06
Myron Towsley

At the end of her freshman year at North Western College, Genevieve asked the Dean of Women if there were any summer jobs for which she might apply. She was told there was one possibility: Naperville Creamery Company had advertised for an "office girl." Her interviewer for that job happened to be my father, Myron Towsley, who would woo the college girl and marry her. In the interview Myron seemed to think Genevieve might not be tough enough for what the job demanded. The only other employees were men, who were likely to be big teasers. Years later, Genevieve recalled that initial interview.

He asked, "Are you sure you want to work here? You know we make butter right outside here. Sometimes the churn overflows and runs in here. You might get your feet full of buttermilk. This is a cement floor; it gets damp in the summertime."

I said, "Don't you want me to work here? I'd like the job. I come from Idaho. My father founded a creamery out there. I used to take the milk from the cow. I'm used to a creamery."

"Well, all right," he said, "if you think you can stand it here."

Genevieve took the job and evidently withstood the sloppy conditions and teasing coworkers rather well; she returned to the creamery the next two summers. She reminisced, "I was the only girl with about 30 men working there. Once I found a mouse in my desk drawer. Believe me, I matured in a hurry! Anyway, I think that's where Myron's and my mutual respect and admiration started." Myron quickly learned Genevieve had "true grit" and would be willing to handle most any situation.

Genevieve performed the expected office duties, but occasionally she was called to the ice cream production area, too. She became quite proficient at cutting long bars of nearly solid ice cream into pint size portions for the brick shaped cartons that would be shipped to ice cream stores in the west suburban area. Myron floated between several positions, including office manager, delivery boy, supervisor, and shop worker. Genevieve noticed him often and he would frequently stop and talk to her.

One day, a cute little girl in a stroller caught her attention. Genevieve learned her name was Betty Towsley. She was Myron's daughter, not yet three. During the following summer, Myron invited Genevieve out for the first time, and she learned he was now divorced from his wife, Avis. Betty was living with her mother and maternal grandparents in Downers Grove, a few miles east of Naperville.

Myron's Story

Myron's father, William Burnell Towsley, and his mother, Cora (Daniels) Towsley, both grew up in Michigan, near White Pigeon. In the late 1880's William Burnell (he enjoyed using both names) secured a position as secretary for Gordon Selfridge, the partner of Marshall Field. Selfridge and Field had founded a grand new department store on State Street in downtown Chicago. Cora married William Burnell in Chicago in October of 1890. They were able to purchase a new two bedroom home on Prince Street in the new Prince Development in Downers Grove. Myron was born in that house on August 18, 1895. Myron's Uncle, Fred Towsley, also lived with the young family; and the Prince Street home soon proved too small. By the summer of 1897, when Myron's sister, Grace, was born, the family had moved to a more spacious Victorian home on South Washington Street. Their third child, Charlotte, was also born in the Washington Street house in 1900.

Myron rarely talked about his childhood or his youth. When he was about four, he stuck his right index finger in the first vacuum cleaner he ever saw. It cut off the end of his finger just past the first knuckle. This never seemed to be a problem for him. He easily learned to type, which served him well later in the army.

One childhood experience we heard about frequently was Myron's baptism. This took place at the Downers Grove Baptist Church on an Easter morning, probably in 1907. Easter was early that year. There was snow on the ground. Two girls were being immersed that same day. There was only one changing room, so Myron was sent home from the church after his baptism to change into dry clothes. His father tossed his overcoat over him as he took off.

Over the years, each time Myron told that story, the snow got deeper, the distance farther, and the March wind fiercer. We thought he must have run close to a mile from the church to his house, probably in bare feet, that cold Easter morning and that the snow was at least six inches deep. Years later, my husband and I went to find the old Towsley home on Washington Street in Downers Grove. It was right across the street from the Baptist church where Myron would have been baptized! Myron's sprint had to have been less than 75 feet. Unfortunately, experiences like this apparently soured Myron on attending church. He was never interested in going to church with Genevieve until he was over 60.

In high school, Myron was on the Downers Grove track team and loved running. Two other members of that team were Walter Fredenhagen and Earl Prince, the men that founded Prince Castle Corporation (the company for which Myron would later be the advertising manager). When Myron graduated from high school in 1914 he enlisted in the army and served in the Rainbow Division in France under Gen. Douglas MacArthur's command in the artillery. Myron's subsequent hearing loss was attributed to his World War I artillery service.

Myron had three skills the army put to good use. He could type, take shorthand and drive a car. It was 1971 before he shared any of the details of his army experience. He told about becoming separated from his unit behind enemy lines in France. After the armistice was signed he stayed on in the occupational forces.

My father seldom talked about himself, and shared very little about his divorce. Avis and Myron had been high school classmates in Downers Grove and married in 1921. I never heard my father blame anybody for the split. I do know that his and Avis's

Myron Towsley and his model T Ford

first baby died, a stress that frequently causes divorce in shaky marriages. On a rare occasion Myron acknowledged that both he and Avis had terrible tempers. Even Betty agreed that hot tempers ran in her mother's family. Whatever the cause, Myron and Avis were divorced by 1926.

Meanwhile...
Assured that Myron was divorced, Genevieve accepted his invitation, and so their courtship began. Conveniently, Myron had a car—a Model T Ford. One of their favorite places to park was on the country road next to St. Procopius College (now Benedictine University) on the edge of Lisle, then a little town just east of Naperville. One evening, they suddenly looked up to see three bearded faces looking through the slightly steamed up windows. Myron rolled down his driver side window. "Good evening, Father," he said sheepishly. "Oh, sorry to bother you," one shyly replied.

In the late 1920s it was unheard of for a lady to share any of an evening's expenses. Myron was quite embarrassed when after a special birthday celebration for Genevieve with dinner at the College Inn and theater tickets in Chicago, his wallet was empty. Genevieve had to pay the cab fare to the depot.

In 1927, Myron proposed. They were sitting on the sofa in front of the big porch window in the North Avenue house, where my grandparents had moved before Genevieve's senior year at North Central. Genevieve and Myron were very much in love. I asked him once what attracted him to Mother. "She seemed so naïve yet so competent," was his answer. He never talked about her appearance, just that she was "such a great girl."

Genevieve's parents were not excited about this relationship. Probably nobody would have seemed good enough for their daughter. But Myron was a divorced man with a child. He was twelve years older than she. His parents had been divorced. Both Genevieve's brother and sister, Merle and Louise, were separated from their spouses with intentions to divorce. Myron didn't have a college degree but had attended Dennison University in Ohio for one year. Genevieve was graduating with high honors from Naperville's college. It probably seemed as though the odds for a long and lasting happy relationship were not in the couple's favor; and Genevieve's parents didn't want any more heartache in the family.

Not wanting to go against her parents' wishes but believing Myron was the man she wanted to marry, Genevieve went to Professor Oliver, her speech professor, and his wife, for advice. Once the Olivers were convinced she truly loved Myron and he loved her, they encouraged her to say "yes."

Their engagement was announced on Valentine's Day 1929 and a home wedding was planned for June 23, 1929. Genevieve described the wedding at their golden wedding anniversary celebration. "I always heard that there was a taboo against a church wedding if someone had been married before and if a person wasn't a virgin. Heaven knows I was a virgin, but Myron had been married before. So I thought it wouldn't be in good taste for me to have a white wedding dress. I had a coral colored wedding dress and it was the 1920s—the flapper style. Remember? Long waistlines and a new length, uneven hem line. Oh, those were the most horrid of styles! That's what I was married in."

There were no pictures of the wedding. Since the wedding ceremony was at home, the room must have been very crowded. The only guest who was present at both their wedding and the 50th anniversary party was my cousin Ted Fredenhagen, Myron's nephew.

He wasn't yet five years old in 1929; he said "I remember all those big people! I didn't know what to do. It was the first big experience I had as a little kid." Ted's mother, Grace, Myron's sister, provided the music at the piano.

A vivid memory for both Genevieve and Myron was what happened as they were leaving the wedding guests. As the bridal couple was dodging rice and dashing to Dad's car, Grandmother Towsley stepped in front of the couple. "Don't forget to bury the garbage!" she said. She apparently chose these parting words because the newlyweds were intending to honeymoon at the Towsley family cottage on Klinger Lake near Sturgis, Michigan. Myron and Genevieve were quite annoyed, but it later became a family joke through the years. When one of us would leave on an extended trip, we would often pull away hearing, "Don't forget to bury the garbage!"

But the happy couple had trouble escaping their doting parents. Mother recalled, "We stayed all night in the Palmer House our first night, and wouldn't you know, my father met us in the lobby the next morning as we were starting for Klinger Lake. I think he wanted to see how I survived the wedding night. They were pretty concerned about that. In fact, they gave us twin beds for a wedding gift." Genevieve and Myron slept in those beds through over 50 years of marriage.

Mr. and Mrs. Myron Towsley made their first home in the rooms previously rented to "college girls" above Bert and Clara's house on North Avenue. Grandma Clara liked being able to keep an eye on Genevieve. But it wasn't long before Genevieve felt Clara was "invading their life." Not only would she tell Genevieve how she should keep house, what she was doing wrong or what she should be doing, she started discouraging her from ever having children.

"So many babies are born retarded," and "Childbirth is so dangerous!" Clara would say. (Perhaps Grandma Clara remembered losing her second baby and this was her way expressing that loss.) Genevieve had had enough. She said that this was the only time she could remember saying, "I wish you'd shut your mouth!" They didn't speak for days. Bert tried to get Genevieve to apologize. It was difficult for both her parents to give up their protective roles.

Myron and Genevieve moved within the year to a little house on North Eagle Street where the rent was $35 a month. This one story house was north of the C B & Q railroad tracks in the development known as Pilgrim Addition. Stories of life in that home were usually happy stories.

Through the years, Myron's quick temper mellowed and he became a very sweet, man. My husband, Dick, tells the best story illustrating this:

"The first real interaction I had with Myron was when Caryl and I were dating. I had heard from several sources that he could be a formidable person, so I sort of stayed out of his way. But we had this occasion in the summertime when Caryl had to be taken to a 4H affair down at the University of Illinois, and I was given the responsibility of driving Myron's car to Champaign and dropping her off. That went well, but on the way home I burned out the main bearing in Myron's vintage Chevrolet. I hitchhiked home and I remember sitting in the hall by the telephone, wondering, 'What could I possibly say?' Figuring, 'Well, this is it,' I called him.

He said, 'Where are you?'

'I'm in Naperville, sir, but your car is in Mazon.' (75 miles away.)

'Oh, really?' I described the knocking and all that. He was very concerned at the inconvenience I'd been put through to hitchhike home.

'And where is the car?' he asked.

I was embarrassed. I couldn't remember the name of the filling station where I'd left it.

'Well, that's ok, there can't be too many filling stations in Mazon.' And it all went very well.

So I was terribly impressed that he obviously was a man who did justly and walked humbly with his God, but he also loved mercy." Dick and Myron developed a deep affection and respect for each other through the years.

Myron was always the gentleman. If he heard a word from his daughters unbecoming a young lady, we were promptly corrected. He was thoughtful. (He always put down the toilet seat!) I heard it said he was a man who smiled with his eyes, not just his mouth. He knew who he was and let others be who they were. Myron Towsley died in October 1985, two months after his 90th birthday. As Reverend Keith Torney said at his memorial service, "He was a common man; in his commonness was his greatness."

07
Family Additions

Genevieve and Myron hoped to have a child soon after they were married. But when she wasn't pregnant after being married over a year, they sought medical advice. A specialist in Aurora gave them the opinion that it was unlikely that Genevieve could get pregnant. Dr. Ed Moser was the couple's family doctor and had kept up on the latest treatments for infertility. He prescribed the usual morning temperature readings but also he performed the additional procedure of inflating the fallopian tubes with air. The treatment succeeded and Myron and Genevieve soon shared the news with their parents that "Dr. Moser did it!" I grew up hearing this exclamation of delight from Mother whenever family or close friends would be talking about birthing experiences. Later when I naively used that phrase to tell Mother's story, it would bring a little chuckle from the listeners and a "pregnant pause" in the conversation.

After she became pregnant, Genevieve was concerned that she knew very little about caring for babies. When she and Myron heard about a single father who was looking for a temporary foster home for his baby daughter, they welcomed Dolores, not yet walking, into their home so Genevieve could gain experience caring for a child. Dolores was part of the family for about six months. Of course, Genevieve and Myron became so emotionally attached that they hoped to adopt Dolores, but her father found arrangements for her care and was able to keep her.

I, Caryl Louise, was born September 10, 1932, in St. Joseph Hospital in Aurora. Naperville would not have a public hospital until the early 1950s.

The next addition to our household was Mother's nephew, Brayton, Louise's son. His mother was having financial difficulties, as many were in the Depression years. Brayton, a likeable, lanky 10 year old, was easy to include in the family circle. Myron would frequently take him fishing on the DuPage River Saturday mornings. He obviously loved being a part of this family. One morning while I was being fed, he announced, "I love her so much I'm going to marry her!" Mother's response was, "You can't marry her; she's your first cousin!" He quickly responded, "No, she's not! I had a lot of cousins in Idaho before she was born!"

Mother made sure that Brayton attended Sunday school at the First Congregational Church where she and Dad were members. She was surprised one morning when she was cutting up a chicken, Brayton asked her to show him the heart. "I don't see Jesus," he exclaimed with disappointment as he viewed the little dark red chicken part. "What made you think you would?" she asked. "Well I heard that Jesus is always in your heart!" was his reply.

Brayton lived with the three of us about a year until his mother was able to manage having him with her when she found a decorator position with a Milwaukee interior design store. Brayton was always a favorite nephew and Genevieve his favorite aunt.

By mid 1934, as the Depression deepened, Mother's father, Bert, lost his job with Robert Gordon and Company. Mother was pregnant again but was very concerned how her parents could possibly manage with no regular income. Myron insisted, "They've got to live with us." So the Braytons and the Towsleys moved to a two flat brick home on the west side of South Washington Street, just south of Aurora Avenue. Bert and Clara moved into the smaller upper flat. Clara cooked on Mother's stove and carried meals upstairs. Mother spoke of these times with mixed feelings. "That was great in some ways and not so easy in others. We had a built-in babysitter and that was wonderful, but I had a very determined father with ideas that didn't always coincide with ours. I remember once he couldn't turn into our driveway without hitting the neighbor's curb. He took a sledgehammer and just knocked out the curb. The next thing we knew, the police were there. When Dad arrived home, he asked, 'What IS happening?' He probably was not pleased to learn that he would have to pay for the neighbor's curb to keep his father-in-law from being arrested. But Dad agreed to pay the cost. Any lingering worries Bert and Clara had about Myron were likely resolved not long after they moved in with my parents.

The neighbor's curb was just one unpredictable expense that put a financial strain on the household. They drove a used Whippet which constantly broke down. Also, there was a stream of medical bills for Genevieve's knee. (Problems with her knee, that started when she was teaching, plagued Mother all her life.) It seemed to her that they could never get ahead.

Mother gave birth to my sister, Marian, on January 4, 1935, in some of the toughest days of the Depression. Years later, I read William Manchester's *The Glory and the Dream*. He described 1932 as "the cruelest year" and depicted the appalling conditions of the Depression. I remember asking Mother how she and Dad had had the courage to have children. She told me, "If you think it was bad when you were born, it was much worse when your sister was born! The next day there was 10% less cash in your dad's pay envelope than there had been in previous weeks. It was his second 10% pay cut."

Ruby was the first college girl who moved in with the Towsley family in 1938. Like other students who would follow, Ruby earned room and board by cleaning, babysitting and helping with other chores. This made a total of seven in the household.

08
Wife and Mother

"I felt one third a woman until I married, two thirds until I had a child, then I felt like a total woman." These were Mother's words to me when I told her I was pregnant with our first child, Philip. She and Myron had a "mutual celebratory" relationship. (Yes, this is a family therapist's description.) He made her feel beautiful. She made him feel better about himself. Being recently divorced hadn't added to his self worth. Mother said that his self esteem was very low when they first met. He remembered his mother as very depressed. Dad had had very little affirmation from his father, whom he believed was hypocritical. While he was superintendent of the Downers Grove Baptist Sunday School he was seeing other women. His younger sister, Charlotte, confirmed this when Mother and Charlotte were in conversation years later.

Genevieve remembered that in the earlier years of their crowded marriage, Myron did his best to just stay out of the way. After Grandpa Brayton died in 1938, Dad was the only man in a houseful of five women and girls. Somehow we managed with just one bathroom. I think he made sure he was the first one up in the morning. If he felt in the way, he would retreat to the small woodworking shop he had in the basement. Mother would keep him connected with calls down the clothes chute. One evening when we were living on Washington Street, she had me ready for bed and told me to tell Daddy goodnight, calling down the chute. "Good night, Daddy," I shouted. He shouted back, "Good night, Sugar!" "He called me Sugar," I told her. "He loves you and thinks you're sweet," she responded. She would orchestrate as much togetherness as she could.

During the later war years, 1943-45, Mother wanted a new stove because her old one had become rather unreliable. She knew they couldn't stretch Daddy's $40 a week paycheck to pay for a stove. If she were ever going to get one she'd have to figure out a way to add some income. Hoping she wouldn't threaten his self-image as a provider, she came up with the idea of selling her home baked goods and presented it to Daddy. Being the good wordsmith that she was, he must have easily agreed, because I remember no objection. By this time, she had become famous for her baking, so every Friday and early Saturday morning the house would be filled with the most wonderful aromas of yeast breads and delicious cakes baking.

It was my job to deliver her products on Saturday afternoons on my bicycle to her four or five customers. When sugar was rationed, she worried what this would do to her new found career. Subsequently, I not only collected the money for the rolls but also the correct amount of sugar she had used in each recipe. This sugar collection didn't seem to be a problem for her customers. They were just so glad to get such delicious pecan rolls or angel food cake delivered to their door. A bonus for Marian and me was getting to eat the scraped out caramel or the angel food cake crumbs that always remained in the bottom of the traditional tubular pan. I also remember occasionally customers would ask her to make a family recipe of theirs for them. Some of those recipes got added to her own collection.

Earlier, in the summer of 1938, Daddy developed a bad case of quinsy. I think this was the name given to the miserable respiratory infection that we would call strep throat today. Mother was relieved and pleased when to distract himself from his misery, he picked up a set of my "toy" watercolors and started dabbling. Finding it fun, he experimented a little more, even after the quinsy had passed. Next came the purchase of some sketch pads and a book or two of instruction. Any free moment he had, he sketched or painted or read how to or talked to someone to learn more, and thus he improved his style and technique.

When he learned that the artist, Ivan Albright, who had created the painting for the movie "A Picture of Dorian Gray" lived nearby in Warrenville, he and Mother drove over to see him one evening. Dad hoped Mr. Albright would give him lessons. He couldn't be persuaded, but when he saw how Daddy studied the paintings there in the studio, Albright told Mother she'd better start looking for work since he could tell the artistic bug had bitten.

When a couple of his paintings were good enough, they drove to Chicago to get them framed. They knew of no framer closer at that time. When the seasoned old framer looked at the watercolors, he commented, "Pretty good!

Pretty good! Better than saloon hanging around!" When his art seemed to take priority over home chores, Mother tried to remember this.

Later, when World War II broke out, the advertising manager for Prince Castle Ice Cream, the former Naperville Creamery, was drafted. Uncle Walter Fredenhagen, the owner, offered Dad the job and the company would pay for art lessons. For at least four years, two nights a week, he would drive to Oak Park and take the Lake Street "L" to art classes in Chicago at the American Academy of Art. It made for long days, but he loved it. I don't think his $40 a week paycheck got any bigger, but Mother was so pleased that he seemed so much happier. His art enlarged their "social circle". Mother enjoyed being with the "tag along spouses" of the Hinsdale Art League or the friends they met the summer when they went to Saugatuck, Michigan, to the Chicago Art Institute's summer school. They became good friends with several of the artist couples.

A big test of their marriage came in January 1951. Part of the advertising manager's job was once a month to put up the "billboards" advertising the monthly feature of "One in a Million malted milkshakes," "Top Hat" sundaes or "Castleburgers." Myron had designed these in the previous months. As Daddy kissed Mother good-bye that morning, he acknowledged he wished he didn't have to be out. Thermometers registered near zero and pavements were icey. In late morning Mother got a call. The cord holding the two legs of his stepladder in position had snapped and had given way under Myron. He had fallen and thought he broke a wrist.

She met him at the hospital emergency room where they learned he had broken BOTH WRISTS. Both arms were put in casts from his fingers to above his elbows. This meant that Genevieve had to do everything for him as one would for a baby: feed him, dress him, and take care of his toilet needs. To get through this crisis took all the patience each of them had. She acknowledged that this was certainly the "for worse" of the "for better or worse" in the marriage vows. After about a week Dad figured out how he could light his cigarette himself from the kitchen stove pilot light, (the stove purchased with Genevieve's baking money). For some foods he learned he could feed himself using a long straight pickle fork. At the time, I was a freshman at the University of Illinois Urbana-Champaign, and was able to get home to help for a couple of weekends and take over the feeding at those times, but Mother took care of all his other needs for the eight weeks he was in the casts.

Recently I was asked what kind of a mother Genevieve was. My answer was "loving and firm." We were expected to do certain household tasks. I remember the first assignment I had was to set the table. Marian's was to put on the spoons. We each received a small allowance, starting with a dime a week. As we got older this went up but so did the number of chores. I was expected to dust the living room furniture and the glass shelves on the landing and to scrub the kitchen floor. Mother firmly enforced these expectations. Of course we were to clean up our plates, pick up our clothes and clutter, go to bed willingly, write thank you notes and "not fight." If we failed to achieve these, we were docked.

Not fighting was the hardest with which to comply. As siblings, Marian and I were inevitably disagreeing. For "time out," I was sent to the basement where there was a coal bin at one end. One time I cried so hard and long, coal started rolling down, giving me quite a scare. That was the last time I "disobeyed" so much that I had to be sent there. On the other hand, whenever we brought home a good grade, fulfilled an obligation, or did our chores especially well we were quickly praised.

As previously mentioned, Marian was born at one of the most difficult times in my parents' lives. They were adjusting to painfully diminishing income as well as smaller living arrangements with more people. Survival was a top priority. The balance of nature and nurture is difficult to define, but for whatever reason, Marian was a shy child, though always cute, bright and loved. I'm sure a naturally extroverted older sister was no help. It also seemed easier for me to meet parental expectations. When she was in third grade she developed a phobia about school, which both Mother and Daddy found very difficult to handle. At the time she was the most painfully shy, Mother was in the hospital for about a week recovering from a hysterectomy. When Dad came to the hospital Mother asked how things had gone that day. He told her of Marian's protest. "I spanked her, kissed her and sent her out the door." Fortunately, Kathryn Fry, (later, Kathryn Holler) was a very understanding teacher at Ellsworth School. This shyness gradually passed to everyone's relief.

If they withheld a privilege and we protested, we might also hear, "It's for your own good." If we hadn't come through on some expectation, I can still hear echoes of an occasional, "How can you do this to me!" When we had done what was expected or gone beyond that, Mother, more than Daddy, would verbally tell us how much she loved us or how proud she was of us. We knew Daddy felt the same way, but as a man of his time, he was less sharing of his emotions.

As I reread my diary from my high school years, I was reminded of the many chauffeuring trips my parents made to get me to out-of-town high school events or 4H events. It was during these times I felt the love and support from both parents, but I don't recall ever telling them that. One event in particular is memorable involving the State Fair in 1947. We were just back from a month-long car trip in the east—a family first. In the mail stack on our return was a letter from Betty wanting to be married "next month" in the Catholic Church in Naperville. (Betty had become a Catholic convert in college. She and Charles Bernardin had met in the registration line for graduate school at the University of Wisconsin the previous summer.) Would the folks give the wedding? It would be a financial stretch, but they wanted to do this. Then we learned I had been selected to go to the Illinois State Fair from DuPage County as a "clothing alternate" in the 4H division. Remembering her own 4H days at the Idaho State Fair, Mother wanted to be sure I got there. So she quickly took care of wedding plans and volunteered to drive a car full of giggly girls to Springfield and to serve as a chaperone for four days. I think she was reliving some of her own 4H joys through Marian and me even though it meant sleeping on lumpy army bunks, lined up 200 deep in the 4H Building at the fair grounds. The wedding went very well. Even though Dad and Mother had planned and paid for Betty's and Charles's wedding, Avis was the bride's mother and so was given that place of honor in the church.

More than once Betty said to me, "I couldn't have had a better stepmother than Genevieve." Up through high school she frequently had Sunday dinner with us and spent the afternoon. She celebrated holidays with us. It was like a special party when Betty was with us. For one semester, Betty was our "college girl." For her college freshman year she enrolled at North Central and lived with us. When she found a way to commute with other Downers Grove students to Naperville, she chose to move out. Mother admitted she ran a "pretty tight ship," which was a difficult adjustment for Betty. Betty didn't want to feel guilty if she wasn't home for supper at a certain time or stayed out later than Genevieve thought she should have.

Through the years the two became very close. After Betty was married, Mother went to Madison to help out when baby Anne was born a month early. There were regular letters or phone calls, which I know Mother treasured. Betty and her husband, Charles, had nine children, so Mother made sure Dad and she went to Pennsylvania at least once a year to visit them.

Betty's mother, Avis, by then a semi-invalid, was living with Betty. During those visits it was not unusual for Mother to help with the housework, including doing laundry and ironing Avis's dresses. When Avis died, Genevieve wrote her obituary for the Downers Grove paper. Never did I hear Mother express jealousy or bad feelings toward Avis, though she was Dad's former wife. She was Betty's mother, and thus a part of her family. When Genevieve could no longer travel, Betty came back to Illinois to see her even after Daddy had died. I remember my husband Dick's mother saying that she was impressed with Mother's and Betty's relationship.

Once we girls had left home, Mother and Dad became closer than they ever had been. Daddy seemed to enjoy helping out with the dishes and other chores. I observed there were more occasional love pats and hugs than I had seen before.

At their golden wedding celebration Mother said, "It seemed like a second honeymoon after the girls were married and Myron had taken his retirement. (He retired in 1964.) "In fact, it was so good, he said one time, 'I didn't know life could be so good.' She continued, "I think it's been a marvelous marriage. One reason was we never tried to fit one another into the other's mold. He'd do his thing; I'd do mine, and we respected each other to always be our own person. He's been so wonderful to let me do all the things I've done, a fact I've told him many times. One time he answered me, 'Well, I wanted a happy wife and I knew if you didn't do some of these things, you wouldn't be happy, and I wouldn't be happy then either.'"

No wonder, when she received the Doctor of Letters honor from North Central College, she declared, "I've always been a liberated woman!"

09
The Depression

Mother acknowledged, "Things were pretty rough for us." Banks had closed, but at least, your Dad was able to keep his job. He was paid in cash. The first payment to come out of that small cash bundle was child support for daughter, Betty, but that left the problem of where to hide the rest. I racked my brain, and one day I was cleaning and I discovered the cold air register. I couldn't think of any other place to put it."

It was not unusual to have a "tramp" at the door after supper, hoping there would be leftovers he could have. I remembered one evening, I was not yet four, when Mother put together a leftover meal of a sliver of meat loaf, baked potato and a sliced tomato for a grateful stranger at the front door.

Genevieve wrote in one of her "Skylines" articles about those years, "The Depression years were ones in which there is no pleasure in remembering…The city's mayor issued a statement in *The Naperville Clarion* stating that "the floating population begging food will be fed night and morning with instructions that if they repeat their visit in town, they will be arrested for vagrancy." A community soup kitchen had been set up. The town was drawn together in a great common concern---survival.

The fact that Dad was able to keep his job with the Naperville Creamery kept them from the receiving line at the Naperville Relief Society. These years were so difficult for Genevieve that for the rest of her life, she was fearful that the family income would suddenly disappear. Her family had gone through severe economic hardship in Idaho. It seemed as if it could be repeated again and again. Shopping was rarely a pleasant activity for her. She seldom bought anything for herself. I can't remember any spending occasion in which she wasn't concerned whether they could afford the purchase—be it some entertainment, dinner out or a new sofa. It wasn't until the early 1960s that she quietly acknowledged, "I realize I can go into a grocery store and buy whatever I want."

I believe she was one of the original recyclers. She would reuse any smidgen of butter left on a dinner plate in her cooking. She had the largest collection of pre-used foil baking pans I have ever seen. "Save the paper!" was always the exclamation when a gift was opened. Later, in my own house in the 1980s, I was finding fragments of holiday paper that I remembered from packages we had opened in the 1940s! By that time I was feeling nostalgic and would reuse the paper to wrap a gift for mother or my husband who might have remembered its first use.

One of the unfortunate effects of the heavy worry about finances was the psychological effect it created on the rest of the family, particularly my younger sister, Marian. More than once she wondered aloud if she had been "a wanted child." All three of us girls, Betty included, carried a spending guilt for many years, longer than was really necessary.

The Depression had a positive effect on mother's cooking. Having less to begin with made her a very creative cook. Some of this was learned in Idaho, but her pecan rolls, her beer braten and her meat loaf recipes were developed out of necessity.

There was no shopping for new clothes. Even Mother wore hand-me-downs from Grace, Dad's sister. The ones I wore were those worn by Rita and her sister Jeanne, Grace's daughters. I was lucky because they were especially nice clothes that came from Marshall Field and Company, where Aunt Grace was given a discount because she was the accompanist for the Marshall Field Choral Society. Marian wore them after I did. Sometimes Barbara and Martha, Merle's daughters, wore them after we did. We did get new shoes when we needed them.

A Soldier Bonus was paid to World War I veterans in 1936. Daddy received $1,576. This made a new house possible, providing the down payment on a house of their own. A new bank, Naperville National Bank, had opened and helped them work out the financing on a Federal Housing Authority (FHA) loan. They bought Arthur Rassweiler's wooded lot in McIntosh Highlands on South Julian Street for the cost of back taxes and special assessments. Payments, the same size as their rent payments had been, were arranged. Emery Meiley, whom Mother said was "highly recommended," was only too glad to agree to be the builder. He had had only one contract during the entire Depression.

Mother wrote in "the Grapevine" on the 40th anniversary of their taking possession of 417 South Julian Street:

"He was delighted to help us choose a plan from his book of plans—one that would meet our needs, our 55-foot lot, and our financial resources. Blithely and quickly we picked a floor plan—a two story house with four rooms downstairs (one to give my folks a private living-dining room) and three bedrooms upstairs. We also requested an attic, a full basement, a fireplace, insulation, and a stoker (to save Myron from frequent shoveling coal into the furnace.)

We let him know the maximum we could spend for a home, and when he said he would build it within that amount, we told him to go ahead. We sought no other bids. We have always been grateful for one of his suggestions. Instead of a frame exterior, he advised we sacrifice the stoker and put the money into brick for brick veneer exterior. Since we converted to gas heat within a few years, the stoker would have been a white elephant. With a minimum of negotiation, specification or delay, Mr. Meiley gave us a well-built house that has pleased us through the years. There are few features we would change.

Early in September, 1936, a teamster, driving a three-horse team, hitched to a scoop-like implement (in Idaho it was called a "fresno"), scooped our basement. One tree had been felled to make room for the dwelling. With the temperature hovering just above zero on moving day in January 1937, we posted Ruby, our student girl, at the door to open it only briefly as the movers carted in our goods. What a great feeling to take possession of our own home!"

Although I was only four and Marian just two years old, I remember the exultation of owning our own home.

10

The Home Front

"Be quiet!" (It was never easy for me to be quiet.) My grandfather's shouting is my first recollection of an impending crisis of war. H.V. Kaltenborn was on the radio with the evening news. It was 1939. All I could figure out was something big was happening in Germany and that Hitler was a bad guy. Then on December 7, 1941 when Japan attacked Pearl Harbor, it was obvious the country was now involved in something terrible. I remember feeling that I shouldn't interrupt.

Both Mother and Daddy worried aloud if he would be drafted. She knew he would willingly join if called. After all, for his vacation in the summer of 1940, he had spent nearly a month at Fort Sheridan in an army refresher experience so he'd be prepared in case he would be needed. It was a good six months after Pearl Harbor was attacked before they were certain that he wouldn't be drafted because he was over 45 and had served in World War I.

Gasoline was soon rationed, so the family now worried how Daddy would get his job done. He had to travel all around Chicago's western suburbs to service equipment at all the Prince Castle Ice Cream stores. He did have a company car. For that, he was granted a "C" card, which meant extra gas. The family car had an A card, with a much smaller allotment. There was worry that even with these, gasoline would be in short supply. Just in case, things got worse, he bought a heavy "balloon tired" Schwinn bicycle outfitted with the largest of baskets, big enough for a toolbox. He installed a three speed coaster brake and large saddle bags on the rear fender. He was prepared! This was his family script, an important learning from his childhood. He never had to use the Schwinn to get to work. He enjoyed it when he took an occasional Sunday ride with the Naperville Bicycle Club, and he and I rode together a few times to Downers Grove, stopping for orange soda pop at a small grocery near Maple Avenue.

The bicycle served him well when he was appointed Air Raid Warden for our block bounded by Julian, Prairie, Columbia and Porter streets. There were black-out drills about every two months, and he would go out on his bicycle to be sure the block was in total darkness. He had a flashlight with the bulb end covered with green cloth, secured with a rubber band so he wouldn't be spotted from the air. We girls could listen to the table Philco radio as long as we covered the glow of the dial with a washcloth. No German bombers were going to see Naperville!

There was a strong feeling in the house that we must do whatever it takes to win the war. There were scrap metal drives, coat hanger drives, grease drives, bond drives, and stamp drives. Mother helped supervise us kids as we went collecting for these to neighbors with our little red Radio Flyer wagon. In addition to gas rationing, there was sugar rationing and meat rationing. These shortages demanded a lot of talk and planning, but I don't remember ever "going without" because of the rationing. This probably speaks well of Mother's good management more than anything else. This was the only time I can remember margarine, we called it oleo margarine, replacing butter on our table. Of course, it wasn't colored and to make it look like butter we had to mix in the envelope of coloring powder that came with it. That was an unpleasant task that I was glad my Grandmother Brayton usually volunteered to do.

While few other items were rationed, many items would be in short supply. My husband, Dick, was a soda jerk at Oswald's Pharmacy then. He remembers that Harold Kester, his boss, forsaw a shortage of chocolate syrup, so he stocked up. The supply allowed them to make chocolate shakes and sundaes clear through to the end of the war. Dick remembers there were a lot of sherbets and ices served because butter fat for ice cream was scarce. Often many of Dad's Prince Castle billboards featured three flavors of sherbet; orange, lemon, lime for a special price. Cigarette deliveries were made to the drug store just once a week and then they were "off brands." The popular brands, like Camels, Lucky Strikes and Chesterfields, were reserved for the military. Neither silk nor nylon was available for making women's hoseiery. I was given a pair of rayon stockings for my 13th birthday (1945) and was thrilled to get them. Since we couldn't get rubber heels for our shoes, the heels we could get of synthetic rubber made black marks on the floor.

Mother and Daddy were not gardeners, but Grandma planted a large vegetable garden behind our garage. I had a small one. Victory gardens were encouraged in Naperville. Vacant land near Merner Field House was plowed, and then small plots were assigned to families to garden. Gardening became a community activity. Several families would be at their patches at the same time and their children would enjoy playing together at the site.

No cars were made for civilians from 1942 to the end of the war in 1945. Synthetic tires were all that were available and they didn't wear well. Our family bought a 1941 Dodge from Clyde Netzley and Company in Naperville the week Japan surrendered in August. 1945.

Naperville, like many of the suburbs, set up a USO collection hut. It was next to Nichols Library. Friday afternoons and Saturdays, volunteers took turns there accepting baked goods or cash that was then taken to Chicago by train late Saturday afternoon. The large USO center in Chicago would distribute these to service personnel. When I delivered Mother's baked goods to her customers on Saturday, I also took a pan of rolls to the USO volunteer hut.

I remember Mother knitting socks and sweaters with a heavy dark khaki yarn for the Red Cross, and once weekly she went to the YMCA where she joined other women rolling bandages. They wore white uniforms and a headpiece that looked like a nurse's cap with a dark blue cotton "veil." As I remember, that was intended to keep hair from falling onto the bandages.

An army program for officer training was set up at North Central College and groups of soldiers were often seen around town. Activated August 9, 1943, it was called the "Army Specialized Training Unit." When they marched as a group from the dorms, mainly Bolton Hall, to campus and back they would be singing military airs. This was all very exciting for an eleven year old girl. A dozen or so kids on bicycles were usually following the singing marching units. A military ball on March 9, 1944 was its final activity in Naperville. From there, troops were sent to active army units.

Mother and Dad had four nephews who were drafted, which created an even higher level of concern about the war. Brayton, Aunt Louise's son, who had lived with us, was in the navy, and later in the war was sent to Saipan in the Pacific. He was the one we had been the closest to, so we hung on to every word of news broadcasts from the South Pacific. His older brother, the one we called Bobby, was in the Army Air Corps. He had been shot down over New Guinea but survived in the jungle. When there were letters from either of these, you could feel the tension in the house diminish.

"Sco"or William Scofield, Aunt Charlotte's son, was in the army but never overseas. Ted, Aunt Grace's and Uncle Walter's son, was in the Marines. He was such a great trumpeter that he was kept stateside to be part of a Marine Band. We all wrote letters to each of them to keep their morale up, and, of course, boxes of Genevieve's home baked cookies were mailed occasionally.

A positive effect of the war for the family was the job change for Daddy. When Don Cooper, Prince Castle's advertising manager, was drafted, Walter Fredenhagen, Prince Castle president, wanted Myron to take over, and he agreed to pay for the art lessons, which would change Dad from an amateur to a skilled commercial artist. Genevieve was pleased with this change because her husband enjoyed his work so much more. Dad faithfully went to classes two evenings a week at the American Academy art in Chicago, enjoying them immensely. It didn't mean much more money, but the job was more pleasant for Dad and a great deal more challenging than repairing ice cream cases or managing building maintenance. When "Coop" returned from the service, he didn't want to return to his old job, which allowed Dad to enjoy being advertising manager even more.

The good news that the Japanese were willing to surrender came on August 14, 1945, VJ Day. I think it was just coincidence that the new, used car, a 1941 Dodge, was delivered from Netzley's that day. It felt like this purchase was in celebration of the end of the war. Naperville's celebration was nothing like those pictured in New York City or Chicago, but bells rang and horns honked. A few girl friends and I got parental permission to ride our bicycles downtown that evening to enjoy the excitement. Cars filled with teenagers were circling on Washington, Jefferson, Main and Benton. Horns were honking and passengers were waving. Of course, we waved back!

11

Vacations

Genevieve's Idaho story told about Brayton family vacations to Yellowstone National Park over very rough roads, having their camping provisions eaten by bears and high prices for camping essentials. None of these seemed to dampen her enthusiasm for a vacation adventure. The only Towsley vacation experience I heard about was "the cottage at Klinger Lake." I can recall no particular memories associated with it. These unshared and apparently much more prosaic vacation reactions foretold the pattern of trips for Mother and Dad through their fifty years of marriage. Mother was always more eager for a trip than Dad. Evidently, there were some weekend stays at a Wisconsin cottage when Grandma Brayton was available to stay with Marian and me when we were under five. The only evidence of these being pleasurable was a couple of small pencil sketches of pine trees and a cabin that Daddy had drawn.

Separate vacations became the norm. The first one I remember was when Mother went to Milwaukee to visit her sister, Louise. She took me along. Louise was eager for her to see the interior design studio she was managing. Her son, Brayton, and I played hide and seek in the studio before it would open in the morning. Slipcovered chairs and floor length draperies made wonderful hiding places.

1940 was the year of VERY separate vacations. Marian and I enjoyed a month with Aunt Evelyn and Uncle Will Kranov, at their farm near Harmon, Illinois. They were the parents of Elaine, who had been one of our college girls. Mother went to Idaho to visit old childhood friends, her nephew Bobby, and a former minister and his family.

Thundering war clouds were evidently booming more than I realized at the time, for Daddy felt an obligation to go to a summer army training program at Fort Sheridan for a month. He could come home on weekends. The following letter, sent to Mother in Idaho, describes the activities of that experience

7:30 pm
July 26, 1940

Dear Honey,

I'm in my tent tonight with one of my knockout headaches. Too much sun, I guess. This week has been terrible, although today wasn't so bad. Also I have a slight cold. One week from tomorrow, in the morning, we leave here. That will be Saturday, August 3rd. Received your card today, dated Wednesday. I had already written asking when you will be coming home.

I met Ethel downtown in front of their store.

I suppose I should be reading Drill Regulations, but, fiddlesticks, there will be plenty of time for that if war comes. There is good reason to believe that if the nation's present preparedness program is carried out, there will not be any war. And, all I can think about is getting home. The camp has been fine. If conditions get any worse I may attend it again next year. But there isn't any active military service in sight for me, I'm glad to say. Whatever duties may come my way in civilian life I will be glad to perform.

Collins and Anderson have gone with Wilson to a Hebrew church service here at the post. He is a Jew. So is Axelrod. I expect to take Collins with me to Naperville tomorrow and then return in the evening. I would like to spend one Sunday in camp.

I just took time out to batten down the tent sides—in the nick of time for it is raining to beat the band. But, tra, la, it has cooled off.

Am anxious to get at my drawing again. Here is hoping I can stay out of the male chorus this winter. But we can talk about all this when we get home again.

I wrote you asking whether I should go after the kids on Sunday, August 11th. Please advise soon as possible.

Axelrod has just come in with some tongue sandwiches he got somewhere. Now will go to the canteen and get a Coca Cola and then really eat!!
Write as often as you can.

Love,
Myron

There were no vacations during the war years that followed, and Dad evidently remembered missing Mother so much that in 1946 we took a family vacation to Klinger Lake. By this time the Towsley cottage had been sold, but we rented a cottage further along the shore. Betty went too. It was a very special time, which provided happy memories. I was taught how to paddle a canoe. Daddy sketched and sketched. The following winter he did a lovely watercolor of Marian from a photo he had taken of her the day we took a family canoe trip up to Middle Lake. Mother remembered that trip because I kept singing, "This Is the Birthday of Jesus," the whole week. She even talked about this at their Golden Wedding celebration. I suspect it was a vacation as close to what Dad had as child as we could have had.

In 1947 the vacation was probably one more like Mother enjoyed as a child. It was a road trip—to New York City and New England. As motels were still uncommon and hotels too expensive, we stayed in tourist homes enroute. Some were good. Some pretty bad. In Shaker Heights, Ohio, one of the good ones, one bathroom was papered with NEW YORKER covers. (I've since used that idea in three separate houses.) A week in Wells, Vermont, living with Mr. and Mrs. Adams was not what a teenager would call glamorous, but I remember it fondly. Mrs. Adams' Grapenut bread is still a family recipe. Daddy painted many wonderful watercolors of Vermont barns and the Green Mountains. Several hang in our home today. Mother seemed to continually be worrying about how much we were spending. When Dad wrote a postcard to the folks back home, the main message was how much driving the trip demanded.

In 1949 the four of us took a 5-day downstate Illinois trip. It is not a trip of happy memories. I don't know if an Illinois Tourism office had been established yet. Aside from the state capitol and New Salem, the places we wanted to visit were closed or empty. The places we stayed always had something unpleasant about them: So much truck noise at Litchfield, and dingy rooms at DuQuoin. We hadn't planned to stay in Decatur, but with ominous black clouds and lots of wind, Dad wanted to get off the road. A modern motel was nearby so the folks decided to pull in there. That was my favorite night, but evidently the folks found it dirty and expensive.

After this trip, the family changed. Boy friends at home, summer jobs, family commitments made things different. Mother grew to enjoy trips more and worry less about money. They took a few trips together but Dad enjoyed travel less and less. For a few years in the late 50's all three of us girls lived in the east, and the folks did drive to where each of us lived, Malvern and Levittown in Pennsylvania and Washington D.C., but there was no real detouring for sightseeing.

A small group of women was planning a trip to the New York World's Fair in 1964. Daddy encouraged Mother to go and have a good time. She did and, of course, wrote a feature story about her experience. In 1969, she wanted to go to Europe. Dad encouraged her to go and have a good time. It was an ocean crossing going over, an air flight for the return trip. She visited four different countries. While she was gone, Dad took the train to California to visit his sister, Charlotte. On his return trip, because of prolonged sitting he developed a pulmonary embolism. By the time Mother returned, Dad was a patient in Billings Hospital at the University of Chicago. While Mother felt a bit guilty, Daddy was so glad he hadn't been expected to go to Europe and that she had had a good time.

The two of them took occasional trips mainly to visit friends and family, but it seemed these had the same undertones: Dad really wishing he were home; Mother worrying about costs.

In 1951 Genevieve's sister, Louise, had remarried and was trying to run a Scandinavian gift shop and furniture refinishing studio near Santa Cruz, California. She needed help and hoped Grandma would come to California to live with her and husband Gus and help out. Grandma was willing. Mother, never having been to California, offered to take Grandma on the train to Louise's. She reserved a berth for Grandma, but to keep it economical, mother rode coach. The sleeper cars were separate cars from the coach cars. One evening, somewhere in Kansas when the train was stopped and there seemed to be a lot of switching going on, Mother casually asked the conductor when he walked through her coach, "Is car 22 still tagging along with us?" "Oh no, Ma'm, that left us about 20 minutes ago back in the yard." A soldier, seeing her plight, grabbed her suitcase for her and ran with her close to a mile to where the sleeper coach was sitting in the yard. She was able to persuade the conductor to let her on car 22, but she would have to pay the sleeper fare. So much for economy! Once she was back in Naperville she wrote a long letter to the appropriate Santa Fe Railroad official about the near catastrophe requesting a refund of the additional fee she paid. Because she had been in a berth for the remainder of her trip, her request was denied. Using the power of the press this adventure made for a great story in *The Clarion*, the first weekly for which she wrote.

She made sure Grandma was well situated with Louise. She made the most of being in California and visited many relatives and friends. She stayed there a few days, enjoying day trips with both friends from college as well as friends from Idaho. Nephew Brayton's family hosted her in the San Jose area. In Carlsbad her sister-in-law, Charlotte, and husband Ben made sure she had a good time. Former Naperville residents transplanted to Los Angeles gave her a warm welcome. In San Francisco, she stayed with Anna, Grandpa Towsley's widow, and her sisters' families. At each home she was graciously entertained and shown the sights. Her letters and cards were filled with superlative descriptions of the lush surroundings and beautiful views.

8:am May 16- "A friend of Louise's took us up to see the giant redwood trees yesterday. They are really impressive. We drove all through the mountains then out on the wharf to get fresh salmon for supper. M-m-good!

Santa Cruz Sun. night 10:30- We had a wonderful drive around San Jose yesterday. We visited the rose gardens—a square block of them—and they are simply magnificent. One just gets overcome with their beauty. There is a high fence around them and on this are gorgeous climbing roses. We also visited the Rosicrucian Museum with interesting Oriental and Egyptian relics.

Wednesday Night May 23—Coming up from Santa Cruz Monday we stopped at Palo Alto and saw the Leland Stanford campus. Yesterday we must have driven 300 miles—across the bay and north into several delightful valleys and over one or two gorgeous mountain passes....

Everywhere she went she was made to feel comfortable and at home, but she wasn't prepared for her experience with Anna's family in San Francisco. Anna was married to Grandpa Towsley for about ten years before he died in 1937. After he died she had moved to San Francisco to be with her sisters, Em and Gertrude, and Gertrude's husband James Hjul. Our family's relationshp with Anna continued to be a close one the rest of her life.

Monday evening at Hjuls'

O-mi-gosh! What an establishment! This James Hjul must be a millionaire. Wish you could see my room--about as big as our living room, all done in the Chinese motif. Twin beds piled high with quilted satin pillows, chartreuse faille draperies, Chinese furniture and accessories. My bath-

room is as big as our bedroom—divided into two parts. One is a dressing room and wardrobe closet; the other is the bathroom proper. It is three steps below my room and of course very ornately tiled in the Chinese manner. I don't know yet how many rooms there are in the place.

I like James-—very genuine and unpretentious. Em and Gertrude are lots of fun and have surely been nice to me. Anna looks well—just as always.

San Francisco –Wed. night May 23

My last night in San Francisco after three memorable days. Yes, they've been wonderful but I'm ready to head south. The Hjuls are wonderful hosts but I will be more at home with the Browns, Loehrs and yes, the Schenks.

As you know the house is built on a hill....I've seen 12 rooms. There may be others. There are numerous porches, balconies, patios, green house, etc. Anyway, I am overwhelmed, especially when the Japanese butler serves my breakfast in bed. They do dress for dinner--I mean the women--but James comes in a crumpled business suit so I don't feel so out of place.

Today Gertrude and I taxied down town and visited Fisherman's Wharf, China Town and the "smart shops." We met Em and Anna at noon but Em and Gertrude had a luncheon date in Oakland, so they went on and Anna and I had lunch at the Fairmont Hotel.

My favorite example of Mother and Dad's relationship and their individual travel tastes is the trip to Mexico. In 1969, Genevieve wanted to celebrate being married 40 years with the two of them taking a trip to that Central American Republic. (Of course neither had been there.) Once again, Dad didn't want to travel but encouraged Mother to go and have a good time. She called on her friends, the Teilags who ran a travel agency, to make the reservations and began to enthusiastically map out her itinerary for a springtime trip. After she received her schedule, Mr. Teilag called to ask her if she would postpone her trip for two weeks. He had to travel in Mexico on business at that time and would be happy to escort her around. She welcomed this service, so the itinerary was moved ahead two weeks.

She was having a great adventure, and all was going well until they got to Mexico City. There they were to stay in a downtown high-rise hotel. It didn't feel any different than a high rise would have felt in Chicago. Genevieve called Mr. Teilag and complained. She wanted to be among the Mexican people, not a bunch of tourists. Mr. Teilag apologized and told her he would make different arrangements after this. Their next night they were in a very rural village where the streets were not paved; there were pigs and chickens below Genevieve's window. "This is more like it," she said, beaming at Teilag when they met for an early dinner in the dining room in the small inn.

Shortly, they were aware of a commotion at the registration desk in the lobby. A couple of women in their

40's were laughing loudly. Then they came into the dining room, smiling, and walked toward Mother and Mr. Teilag. When they came closer to their table, she recognized the faces as familiar. The women identified themselves. Yes, they'd met before. They were the daughters of May Watts, a friend of Genevieve's in Naperville After sharing their mutual amazement to come so far and find someone they knew from their hometown, one turned to Mr. Teilag and said, "We've never met Mr. Towsley!" With amusement, Genevieve explained they still hadn't met Mr. Towsley and how she happened to be traveling with Mr. Teilag. When she returned home she could hardly wait to write this story in her column in *The Naperville Sun*. The best defense is a good offense! Once again Myron said he was glad he didn't have to go and that she had had a good time.

As Daddy began to fail, Mother curtailed further travel until after Daddy died. That was in 1985. The following summer she drove by herself to Springfield for an Elder Hostel trip and in the fall of '86 flew to California to see friends and relatives once more. Of course, each of these provided her with inspiration for her weekly feature story, *Skylines*, in *The Naperville Sun*.

❋ 12 ❋
The Clarion Years

On March 11, 1948, I wrote in my diary, "Mom got $12.30 for her articles in the paper."

Earlier that month, Mother went to downtown Naperville to run errands. She stopped in the newspaper office to renew her subscription to *The Naperville Clarion*. It was the town's oldest newspaper, having been founded by David Brown Givler, a Civil War veteran. James Givler, a great-grandson of the founder, who now ran the newspaper, was in the front office. Later in life, Mother recalled the conversation went something like this

"Good Morning, Jim."

"Oh, hello," Mr. Givler replied. "How are you? What can I do for you?"

"I've come to renew our subscription," Mother said unenthusiastically.

Once she had his attention, she decided to express her disappointment about the current state of the weekly newspaper.

"You know, Jim, there's almost no news in *The Clarion* these days."

"Oh, I know there isn't," was his faint response. Mr. Givler, a short man of slight build, was quite shy, so it's no wonder he said, "I can't get away to get any."

He looked thoughtfully at Genevieve who he knew was a former English instructor at the college. And then he made a suggestion that was to change Naperville's history for the next 40 years.

"Why don't you write us some personals?" he asked.

Because of her disappointment in the contents of the newspaper, her response was noncommittal, when she replied, "I'll have to think about that."

Later that evening, she talked it over with Dad. The more she thought about it, the more she wanted to accept the offer. She loved the English language and having extra income was important to her so she could help provide for the family that included Dad, my sister, Marian, my Grandmother Clara Brayton and me. Always wanting her to be happy, Dad encouraged her to give it a try.

She returned to *The Clarion* offices the next day and a pleased Mr. Givler agreed to pay her the whopping sum of 15 cents an inch. Because Mother was quite active in the community, finding news did not present a problem for her. She was always interested in other people, which made it easy to find material. The following week she wrote items about news that she had heard at church, at the grocery store, at North Central College or the Book Club. If the news she gathered was not from the original source, she always phoned the subject for verification and asked his or her permission to put it in the paper. A good journalist, she always double-checked her sources. Not knowing how to type, she turned in her stories in longhand. Mr. Givler accepted whatever she wrote. When he started receiving positive responses to Genevieve's work, he asked her to write a feature story for the next week's edition of the newspaper.

I wrote in my diary, March 16, 1948, "Mother's going strong on *Clarion* news." In an entry dated two days later I had written, "Mother had her first 'We Salute You' column in *The Clarion* today."

This soon-to-be-popular and regular feature was previewed by Mr. Givler in his column, "Town Talk." Mother's first story was about Genevieve Munger, a transplanted Oak Park businesswoman, who was living in Naperville. A relative newcomer to Naperville, she was very interested in helping young girls learn to sew and to develop their full potential. She organized a "girls' group," which I joined. It was called Na-Hi-Co, for Naperville High Coeds. We would meet once a week at her home, bring a sewing project, and generally discuss "girl things." Mrs. Munger was very skilled at clothing design as well as sewing and quickly was in business, designing and making wedding dresses in her home for many Naperville brides. In time this led her to planning entire weddings. Mother's story on Mrs. Munger generated a number of compliments for the writer and also generated additional business for the entrepreneurial seamstress.

Feature stories are "the icing on the cake" for newspaper reporters, but when natural disasters strike in a small town, it's all hands on deck and everyone on a newspaper staff pitches in to cover—even freelance writers. Shortly after Mother started working for *The Clarion*, Naperville was flooded by spring rains, which wreaked havoc on the community. On March 19, 1948 I wrote in my diary, "We couldn't get to school because of awful floods. Huffman Street kids got to school with row boats. Our basement had 22 inches of water."

The Clarion featured lots of news about the flood, but Mother covered the humorous side of the crisis. In her feature of March 25, 1948, she described the town's spirit in spite of the crisis. Les Schrader and Al Biedelman (she called them Naperville's jesters) decided to lend a hand, floating Al's canoe to offer transportation. Les, an experienced sign painter, who also worked for the town's major employer, Kroehler Manufacturing, quickly lettered an appropriate advertisement "Huffman Lake Boat Service." Al was in the masonry contracting business. Many of the children who lived along Huffman Street were ready to climb aboard Al's boat to attend school after the novelty of the flood wore off, and they realized they'd have to spend the day in a cold house because the electricity was out. Les and Al escorted them to school via boat. For years, when a heavy rain occurred, Huffman Street would flood because it was at the bottom of a high hill that led up to the Ss. Peter and Paul Cemetery. Rain would run down the steep incline causing huge problems when it reached Chicago Avenue which did not have enough drainage capacity to accommodate the rushing water.

During the flood, Les and Al also assisted tow trucks with long ropes to remove inundated cars, hoping they could get them out before they were completely soaked. Evidently, they developed a friendly competition with the local firefighters when both pulled alongside Glen Parker's front door to pick him up. Glen owned a local radio store, and much to the jesters' chagrin, he chose the firemen's boat. Al yelled, "I'll never buy another radio from Parker. He's giving his service to a rival concern. Unfair to organized labor!" And so another chapter in Naperville's history ended on a humorous note.

By March 25, 1948, both of Mother's columns had titles. Her feature story was called "Story of the Week." This gave her the freedom to write on a wide array of subjects, not just about a person. Some of her subjects included controversial social issues, along with interesting groups, historic Naperville, and homes of distinction. Her column on personal, human interest items was given the title, "Party Line." Mother's first "Party Line" story told how a child's illness actually played a part in the flood rescue. In this excerpt from the March 25, 1948, *Naperville Clarion*, Mother's column stated "Dickie Raddock's measles were responsible for arousing many of the Huffman Street residents and warning them of the flood! Mrs. George Raddock was up with her son in the night when she discovered water swirling about her home. She called George and he phoned the neighbors to give the alarm."

Mother began to use her *Clarion* columns to welcome newcomers to Naperville, describing the families so that her readers would want to meet them in person. These were interesting families, and often ones who were quite different from the traditional Naperville citizen.

Mother was keenly interested in many different areas and highlighted subjects that ran the gamut from the controversial to the everyday that most of us take for granted. For example she wrote a story about the public school janitors. At that time, most of Naperville's residents had some connection to one of the public schools, even if they had earlier attended a parochial grade school. Many had fond memories of their school janitor. So Mother went behind the scenes to learn what a public school janitor did.

In her subsequent article, she pointed out how conscientious each had to be and how they did so much more than sweep the rooms and run the heating plant. They had to have an understanding of a number of trades to keep the plumbing and electrical equipment in good running order. In the winter, they had the dirty job of shoveling coal into stokers each day. When schools were on vacation, the janitors performed major housecleaning and painting operations. Janitors at the grade school even rang the bell to call children in from the playground.

In her October 28, 1948 "Story of the Week" Mother profiled each of the school janitors. If you lived west of Center Street in Naperville, you went to Naper School. You attended Ellsworth School if you lived east of Center and you probably jumped over Mr. States' wide floor mop or had his help getting your locker open.

All were described but she wrote the most about Mr. States, who had been a custodian longer than any of the others. In 1930, Fred States gave up his job as upholsterer at Kroehlers, the local furniture factory, to become janitor at Ellsworth School. When Mrs. States died in 1932, he was left with five children to parent, the youngest a boy being in kindergarten. Fortunately, he had two older girls, who helped raise the other children. When we would begin to eat our sack lunches in the Ellsworth School gym, I remember seeing the States children hurry into the school kitchen where Mr. States and the older girls fixed lunch.

The family was thus able to eat lunch together at Ellsworth School, then hustle back to their respective schools.

Mr. States always had infinite patience and a smile on his face. He was never too busy to help us remove a stubborn pair of galoshes or any other task that challenged grade school children. In the mid-1940s, he left to become an upholsterer at Brown's, a children's furniture factory in Naperville, but after two years he returned to remain Ellsworth's janitor for the rest of his career. Merrill Gates, the principal, told how Fred States was welcomed back. He described Mr. States as adding contentment to teachers and students while giving so much attention to appearance details in the building.

Some of Mother's stories drew attention to local people and events, which had national significance. She wrote about Wil-O-Way Farms, describing why it was a world famous enterprise. Prior to this article few in Naperville were aware that Wil-O-Way Farms was much more than just another dairy farm along Aurora Road. After the story appeared the number of school visits to the model milking parlor shot up.

Here is an excerpt from Mother's November 4, 1948 feature.

> *"Nowhere in America will you find a more modernly equipped dairy barn than on the Wil-O-Way Farm two miles west of Naperville. If you have never visited the milking parlors of this famous dairy farm, you have truly missed an enlightening experience. Guests from every state in the union, besides Canada, Brazil and Russia, have signed their names in the several registers which have*

> been filled since the opening of the barn in 1944. The Russian delegation spent two days studying the methods and equipment which George Polivka has developed after years of study and devotion to the dairy business."

After describing in vivid detail the many unique features of the operation, an invitation from the Polivkas was given to the public. Mother explained how one could drop in at milking time any afternoon at 4:30pm and see them in operation. Special provisions were made for visitors in the observation room which was elevated and yet entirely separated from the parlors themselves by glass block windows. She called it "one of the most interesting shows in the country." Later in November those of us in the Cheery 4H Club had signed our names in the register. We were not disappointed.

Mother didn't have an office, per se. Her space for writing was at the bookcase secretary in the living room at 417 S. Julian Street. It was the style of desk that had a "fall front." It pulled down to become a flat writing surface or of course it could be closed and used to cover up partly finished projects. There was just one phone in the house, an ordinary black dial phone, typical of the times, and that was in a corner of the kitchen. Mother would shuttle between the phone and the desk. There was usually a stack of scratch paper on the counter beside it, along with a few pencils of varying lengths. She would scribble notes and later use them to jog her memory as she wrote her "Party Line" column.

Because the *Clarion* came out on Thursdays, Mother would write all day Mondays and on Tuesday mornings. Tuesday afternoon she delivered her week's work to the *Clarion* office on South Washington Street, which was located in a cluster of historic buildings a few doors south of Jefferson Avenue. When I was home on school vacations, I'd go along with Mother and run into the office with the week's work. It was a typical newspaper office, cluttered, a bit dusty, with stacks of recent weekly issues piled around. The aroma was that of an oily paint. In mild weather, she'd trust me to deliver her stories on my bicycle.

On writing days we often saw her with the phone in her left hand at her ear and a pen in the right. If we were at home on those days, we were expected to stay off the phone. We learned not to expect her to be available for school field trips or 4H events on writing days. (This wasn't difficult for us.) On the other days of the week, she had interviews, usually one or two a week. Many evenings after supper, she would be back at the living room desk finishing up a weekly feature.

One summer in the early 1950's, North Central College offered a short typing course to the community. Mother signed up and learned quickly, which allowed her to submit typed articles for most of the rest of her writing career. She would type out her articles and columns on a black Underwood typewriter, the clacking of the keys echoing throughout the house. It certainly cut down her writing days significantly and allowed her to more effectively produce her columns which were becoming increasingly popular with the public.

Mother loved her interviews. They were frequent topics of dinner table conversation the evening after she'd met with her interesting subjects. By the end of those evenings I felt our family's friendship circle had widened considerably. Her favorite interviews were those she had with Naperville's older residents. She particularly appreciated Eli Stark, former toy shop owner and budding experimental photographer, for his good memory and fascinating stories. Mr. Stark had created unusual photographs using a unique dual image technique, such as one where it appeared as though he was boxing with himself. Up until that time I knew him only as the man who ran the only taxi service in Naperville.

On Sunday afternoons, I was a volunteer guide at the Martin Mitchell Museum those first years Mother was writing. The museum was housed in the former Martin family mansion, which with its surrounding 212-acre grounds had been willed to the City of Naperville by Caroline Martin Mitchell, the last member of the family. The Naperville Heritage Society, which now administers the home, wouldn't be a reality for another 15 years. I like to think that my enthusiasm for the museum contributed to her interest that first year she was writing. She and I went out one evening with Bertha Finkbeiner, Mrs. Thomas Finkbeiner, who was then the curator, for Mother to "get a story." It was while she was researching the Martin Mitchell story that she learned of the gold mine of historic material stored in the cupboards of what had been the maid's bedroom.

At least once a month for several years, with tote bag in hand, filled with the sheets of leftover paper from the *Clarion* printers, and number two pencils, she would head to the museum. She'd spend an afternoon going through crumbling newspapers, official town documents, or occasionally, old letters, making notes furiously, then bring them home to the living room desk to compose a story about the Napers or the Hobsons or the Naper Academy.

Originally, Mother never thought of herself as an historian. She would say she was a journalist who was after a good story. It wasn't until she'd been writing over ten years when she realized that the articles that brought the most comment were her features on historic Naperville. At that point she acknowledged that she had become an historian.

She also would not identify herself as a social activist, but her articles on social justice issues reflected her social conscience. In the fall of 1949 she had spent a day with one of the DuPage County Department of Public Aid social workers visiting the many places in which the indigent county residents lived. One of the stops that day was the recently modernized County Convalescent Home. She turned that day's experiences into an enlightening Story of the Week. Later in the month, that day's experience, the power of the pen and Genevieve's persistence paid off.

In this story from *The Naperville Clarion*, dated October 27, 1949, she talks about a Naperville resident whose limited pension and mental illness caused him to become homeless. Mother navigated the confusing web of social services to finally find him a home.

"No home. No family or friends. Past eighty and becoming more incompetent mentally each day, this was the plight of John Krause last Friday. He is an example of that ever growing population of wandering old people who present a difficult problem to our welfare organizations. John Krause receives $80.00 a month from his Social Security check and Old Age pension, but that is not sufficient to pay his way in a nursing home. He was asked to leave each of the several rooming places which he formerly occupied in Naperville. Last February, while the John Fender family was absent from their home, he moved his belongings and himself into their house. Mrs. Fender, who has known him for years didn't have the heart to turn him out."

This turned out to be a short-lived arrangement since his behavior was so disturbing. When Mrs. Fender tried to get him into the County Convalescent Home, she was given the predictable excuse, "We're overcrowded" and there's a long waiting list." When Mrs. Fender consulted with the State's Attorney's office in Wheaton, she was told she could either commit him to Elgin State Hospital or put his belongings in her front yard. Mr. Krause told her he'd made other arrangements so she was relieved, but when the "other arrangements" didn't work out, the cab driver took him and his baggage to the taxi station and left him there.

Mother learned of the situation when a friend phoned her urging her to test the various county organizations for help. At 10:30 am, she went to the cab stand and found the bewildered Mr. Krause. He gave her permission to call the Lisle Township supervisor. Because the supervisor wasn't home, his wife Mrs. Kletzche, suggested Mother call his case worker, Mrs. Van Burkem. Mrs. Van Burkem expressed doubt that he could be placed at the home in Winfield. Mother insisted that as long as the home was not filled to capacity, he should be accommodated. She was very glad she had recently visited the institution and was familiar with its conditions.

At 2:30 p.m. that afternoon, Mother received a call from Mrs. Van Burkem from the Courtesy Cab Station.

Miss Deverall, the matron of the county home had accepted him for placement. Mrs. Van Burkem had driven to Naperville to pack up Mr. K., received his authorization that he was a resident of Lisle Township and taken him to Winfield.

In her article, Mother complimented Mrs. Van Burkem. "Such quick work and efficiency on Mrs. Van Burkem's part was almost unbelievable and most gratifying." It turns out Mr. Krause had been a Mason for 30 years. Mrs. Van B. planned to contact the lodge to which he belonged and arrange for a transfer to the Illinois Masonic home as soon as possible. Mother's pen proved to be quite powerful in providing solutions to problems that others would not even tackle or even hope to solve.

Mother continued to write about interesting people, interesting places, interesting events. She was always a little surprised at the compliments she would get on her columns. "I thought what you wrote about Charlotte Marouse was so thoughtful." "The junior class was glad for the boost you gave to their off-campus prom plans." "That was sure interesting what you wrote about all the Haas boys and their baseball team." "I didn't know we'd had a cigar factory in Naperville, let alone that Judge Knoch had worked there!" She created a feeling of inclusiveness as she wrote about everyday lives, making them seem special.

She frequently said, "I couldn't write fiction. I have to write about what I know." The fact that she did that so well was proven when the Illinois Press Association named her Story of the Week about Professor Guy Oliver "Best Feature Story" of the year in October 1952 in its annual competition. The Illinois Press Association judges wrote, "Writer turned routine story of professor's retirement into

Genevieve Writing

warm and revealing portrait using incidents and anecdotes to delineate character drawing on her knowledge of the subject, but avoiding excessive sentimentalism. She seems to catch the essence of the man and affections with which he is regarded."

The original story had been published May 15th that year. In it Mother acknowledged that "Professor Oliver is one person about whom I cannot write objectively." He was an important influence in Mother's life and offered her encouragement throughout her college career and even after graduation. He is the one to whom she asked for his opinion about her marrying Dad. Without being "syrupy" she wrote a touching "I remember" feature about the beloved professor, Professor Guy E. Oliver, who had been head of the Speech Department at North Central College, for 36 years and was planning to retire at Commencement time. She acknowledged she couldn't appraise him as a stranger might.

The first time she saw him, she was disappointed in his appearance. She noticed he was short, balding and had a scar on his face—not what she had pictured about this man about whom she had heard so much. He was making an announcement from the chapel stage, and with his first words that impression was erased and his warm personality shone through.

Prior to the first speech she gave in his class, she recalled that she was trembling both outward and inwardly. After the speech, he handed her a sheet of constructive comments. Below these he had written, "Mine for the gold that is within you!" What a confidence boost for this shy Idaho girl!

She easily recalled many of his classes. He taught the value of "positive suggestion" among his many practical ideas for everyday living. She could recite almost word-for-word a chapel talk of his that began, "If I had it to do over again I would never fall in love." Then after a brief pause he exclaimed, "I'd DIVE in!" the whole talk was a celebration of a happy marriage and an indirect tribute to Mrs. Oliver.

Mother described how the Oliver family, including children, Jean, Guy Jr. and Donnie, included many of the students in family activities. When Donnie died with an incurable blood disease, the students felt as though they had lost a family member.

In retrospect, it must have been a relationship of mutual admiration. He was so proud of her when she took second place in the national Oratorical Contest. Before she graduated, he asked her to be his assistant. Those two years as an instructor were very pleasant for her. When she had to be out for seven weeks to recover from knee surgery, he took over her classes, refusing any compensation for it. In the late 1930s Prof, as she called him, directed a community theater play, "the Family Portrait," about the life of Christ. Although she had only a bit part in it, Mother recalled the thrill she felt being directed by him again. In 1950, they collaborated in writing the history of the Royal Arch Masons, a lodge of the Masonic order, on the occasion of their 100th anniversary. Many North Central students had similar warm feelings for him. She closed the column quoting the lovely tribute to him in the 1941 *Spectrum,* the college's yearbook. At that time he had been on campus 25 years.

"Here is a man with a thousand voices...developed by his teaching. Here is a man with a thousand minds...cultivated by his thinking.... Here is a man with a thousand philosophies...off-springs of his principles. His appreciation of the high ideals exemplified in the masters of the past has kindled within his personality the spark of inspiration. This spark has struck a flame to the ideals of past students and spreads like a prairie fire among the students of today. This little man has taught us to speak. He has challenged us to think and inspired us to the point of action. His friendly sincerity has aided us in our search for adjustment. His personality and philosophy have made us admirers. This man shall never die. His influence will have immortality in the lives of his students."

Mother wrote for the *Clarion* for over six years, continuing both her columns and occasionally a third one, "With the College Crowd," about Naperville students attending college. In June 1954 she learned The *Naperville Clarion* had been sold to a Chicago publisher. While wondering if she'd have a job with a new editor, she got a phone call from Vic Thornton, a former co-worker, who now worked for the new paper, *The Naperville Sun*. She was also contacted by *Sun* publisher, Harold White, who had been her student at North Central. Both encouraged her to join the *Sun* family. That ended Mother's *Clarion* years. Two years later the Clarion was out of business, and the oldest newspaper in Naperville closed its doors forever. But Mother's career with *The Naperville Sun* was just beginning, and it was here she was to make her mark on Naperville's hearts and history.

{ 13 }
Naperville Sun Beginnings

It was 1954—an eventful year for the Towsley family. In February Dad had broken both wrists when a stepladder gave way as he was hanging billboards for Prince Castle. It had been a long recovery, with halucinatory side effects from the pain medication.

Grandma, Clara Brayton, seemed to be stable with her heart condition. In the middle of May, suddenly, her situation demanded an emergency trip to Aurora to St Joseph Hospital. When she heard the doctor tell her she had a bowel blockage and surgery would be necessary, her reply was, "Don't you try to save my life. I want to go and meet my sweetheart!' And so she died peacefully. We all felt the loss. The funeral was a celebration of her life.

June arrived. Mother and Dad were truly surprised when dinner out with two other couples turned into a forty-guest surprise party for their 25th wedding anniversary on June 23rd. The next excitement was my graduation

Genevieve, Caryl, Marian, Myron Towsley

1954

from the University of Illinois in Urbana-Champaign. It was a long trip down and back for one day, but the ceremony put an exclamation point on four wonderful years. It also meant no more 4H House bills or tuition payments. Wedding excitement was mounting for Dick's and my wedding to be in August.

"Do you know a Genevieve Towsley who writes for The Clarion?" This phone inquiry interrupted Aunt Grace's small June luncheon that she was hosting at the Fredenhagen Hilltop Farm. The caller was Philip Maxwell, one of the promoters of the Chicago Tribune's annual Chicagoland Music Festival. Aunt Grace Fredenhagen, Dad's sister, was an accomplished pianist and choral director of the YMCA Men's chorus. She knew Mr. Maxwell from when her Naperville Women's Club Chorus had given an award-winning performance at the festival.

Grace told him of the coincidence that Genevieve was her brother's wife and was actually visiting her at that moment. He continued in a rather dictatorial manner,

"I've just bought the *Clarion*." "Tell your sister-in-law to meet me at your house tonight. I want to ask her to be my editor." When Aunt Grace returned to the dining room with the message, Mother was flabbergasted! (Her own word for this experience.) This was the first she had heard that the Clarion was changing hands. She also knew that she wanted no part of editing. She didn't have the interest or the experience to become an editor. She enjoyed writing her columns and features.

She did meet the Maxwell family that evening at the Fredenhagen home. She politely thanked Mr. Maxwell but told him of her decision. His jovial manner changed abruptly when she told him she only cared to be responsible for her writing assignments. This was a response he didn't anticipate. "Well that being the case, I'm not sure we'll need your services any longer," he said with a dismissive gesture.

As she drove home she wondered if she still had a job. She decided to stay away from the Clarion office and await developments. She would wait a week. If she hadn't heard from Mr. Maxwell within the week she thought she might ask Harold White, *The Naperville Sun* editor and publisher, to find a place for her on *The SUN* staff.

She didn't have to wait that long. Two days later Vic Thornton, a former Clarion colleague, who had switched to *The Sun*, called. "We hear the *Clarion* has been sold. Harold is wondering if you might now consider coming with us." Trying to be casual she replied, "I'll be glad to talk about it." Within minutes Harold called asking if he could come over that evening to discuss a possible agreement.

That call came as she and I were getting ready to eat a lunch of leftover chop suey. As she sat down to eat, she knew she was going to agree to write for *The Sun*. The enormity of this decision was starting to sink in. "What have I done?" she wondered aloud. That was a call that indirectly led to changing Naperville history.

Harold arrived that evening. They worked out a satisfactory arrangement. She would write four columns: a feature, and a column of human-interest items, (like Party Line had been), "With the College Crowd," and a column of personals. He offered to pay her double the amount she had been receiving at *The Clarion* for the same amount of work.

The following Monday she arrived at the Sun office in mid morning as the staff paused for their ritual coffee break. The circle was widened and immediately she felt welcomed as part of *the Sun* family. They became a pseudo family. Fannie White, Harold's mother, ran the office. She answered the phone, made out bills, took in news and classified ads and subscriptions. Harold, as editor was, involved in every aspect. Eva, his wife, sold ads, made up advertising "dummy" (draft pages) and helped make up the paper. Vic Thornton and Gwen Stiefbold comprised the editorial department. She also wrote the "Flowers for the Living" feature. In addition, there were three or four men who ran the Linotype machines and the presses. The Whites had been her friends ever since she had taught English those two years after she graduated in the department that was chaired by Harold White senior. When he would meet her on the street after she had started writing for *The Clarion* he would comment, "Genevieve, you should be writing for Harold at *The SUN*. You're part of the family." Since *The Clarion* had given her the opportunity to write, she had previously resisted these overtures.

Three days later Mr. Maxwell phoned again. He hoped she would continue to write for *The Clarion*. She admitted that it gave her some satisfaction to tell him she had already become a member of *The SUN* staff.

The first feature she wrote for *The SUN* concerned the avalanche of comic books on the local news stands. She thought much of the subject matter as well as the language used in them were objectionable. Violence seemed to be a prevailing theme. She made a survey of Naperville's four drugstores, the main purveyors of magazines. The town's population was only 7,000 then, so this was easy to do. She discovered that several of the druggists screened the comics that arrived weekly before putting them out for youngsters to purchase. Others made no attempt to control the quality of subject matter. It was features like hers that led to the formation of the voluntary board, the Comics Code Authority.

Within the week, Harold White had named her feature column, "Skylines". He had been impressed earlier by a view of the city from the east, at sunset and snapped a photo of it. From the photo, a graphic artist produced the headline that was used for over forty years.

Genevieve named "The Grapevine" herself. A frequent expression in the family had been, "I heard it on the grapevine." This meant, "Someone told us some tidbit that had been told to them." She may have heard it on "the grapevine" but she always checked out the source for accuracy.

Her first *Naperville SUN* article to cause change was the one that resulted in integration of Centennial Beach. Very late in August, 1954, North Central College was the site of one of their church sponsored conferences. Participants at conferences had earlier been promised that free swimming at the Beach would be one of the activities available. Usually non-residents had to pay. When African American participants at the conference were told swimming privileges were not open to them and that it was a beach policy that "Negroes were not allowed," the conference director called Mother to tell her about the situation. He asked if she had known about this policy. She had not and was outraged.

She raised the issue with the Mayor Wellner who agreed it would become an agenda item at the next city council meeting. It was scheduled for right after Labor Day, just at the time Mother and Dad had reserved a cottage in Wisconsin for a long weekend to "recover" from a long summer. She didn't insist but hoped that Dick and I would attend that council meeting (We were living in the Towsley house for the interim until Dick had to return to medical school at the University of Chicago.) She had learned that some townspeople were circulating a petition to leave beach policies as they were. She phoned the pastors of the churches where each of the council members attended, encouraging them to be present at the meeting. A packed crowd of observers was at that meeting. Dick and I were among them. The council members came into the chambers, above the old city hall on Jefferson Street. Each went to his usual seat. Each pastor was seated where his parishioner would be facing him directly. Discussion was heated. One member voiced his disgust that this *SUN* writer had the gall to tell Naperville government what to do. The council was pressed to produce a copy of "the policy." There was no policy to be produced. It was a "general understanding." With this attention to the situation some councilmen chose to say it was "a misunderstanding," and that people of color could swim at "The Beach". And so they were officially admitted without further question, a great piece of social engineering by a woman of principle who knew the town!

Harold White also attended that meeting as an observer. There was little in the next issue of the paper except in Harold's weekly "Ramblings" column. Harold's lead sentence was, "If Christ were alive today, he'd be crucified." He totally supported Genevieve's writing, that week and every week for the next 40 years, never editing what she wrote, even if he wasn't in total agreement with her.

✹ 14 ✹
The Journalist Becomes An Historian

Mother didn't plan on becoming an historian. Each week she wanted to write an interesting feature of special interest to Naperville's residents. That feature was usually about a unique citizen, an unusual business or a little-known institution, past or present. She had a knack for writing about the ordinary, convincing her readers it was extraordinary, and in addition, to noting how fortunate Naperville was to have that citizen, business or institution as part of the community.

I don't think Mother would be celebrated as an historian today if it hadn't been for Margaret "Peg" Sproul who was then senior editor at the *Naperville Sun*. She and Mother had enjoyed each other's friendship even before they became co-workers at the newspaper. Through the years, Mother had privately hoped that someday her historic articles might be put into a book, and it was, ultimately, Peg whose energy and "know how" made this happen. Even then it was providence the book was published at all. The original copies of Mother's historical articles had landed in a trashcan, instead of going to the bindery. It was a custodian who questioned if that were where they belonged. He caught Peg's attention and the historic writings were saved.

At the time, in the mid-1970s, the nation's Bicentennial was coming up, and there would not be a better way to celebrate Naperville's part in history than to have a selection of Mother's historic articles put into a book celebrating the city's past. With encouragement from publisher, Harold White, Peg took on the project.

Over the next two years, the book consumed a major part of Peg's time as she took on the many tasks of editing. She tracked down old pictures, located duplicates, and wrote captions and headlines, in addition to negotiating with artists, typesetters and printers. She also handled all the financial aspects involved in the distribution and sale of the final publication.

It is comforting and gratifying for me to read in her editor's comments in the introduction to *A View of Historic Naperville* that the book provided her with the greatest satisfaction of her career. Peg had selected 10 of the historic features from the *Clarion* years spanning 1948-1954 to be included in the first edition. Later editions added three more from her *Clarion* years. The rest of the selections were all from her features in the *Naperville Sun* from 1954-1975.

Mother's *Clarion* feature column at first had the title, "We Salute You," but I recently found a browned-from-age clipping of her other column, "Party Line," with a crumbling date of April 22, 1948. In "Party Line," she explained that the new title of her column would be "Story of the Week." Apparently, the reason for the name change was that the word "salute" implied "eulogize." She had been writing less than a month and already had some possible subjects shy away from being interviewed because they felt embarrassed. I remember hearing the disappointment in her voice that first year when an interview request had been refused, perhaps because of the column's original name. As I remember, once the name was changed, people were more receptive. She had consulted with *Clarion* Editor, Jim Givler, to help decide on the new title that would allow her a much wider range of topics -- not only personalities, but also unusual organizations or events in Naperville's history.

What was her first historic piece? Of that, I can't be sure. Many of the early *Clarion* articles I have in my possession were just the articles themselves, many without margins, dates or page numbers. My maternal grandmother, Grandmother Clara Brayton, had clipped those early columns to save her daughter's words, not thinking the dates would be equally important. On just a few, Grandma had penciled the publication dates in her beautiful "Spenserian" handwriting. If the article went on to a second page, that page was attached to the first with a straight pin. Since my grandmother was a talented seamstress, she had an ample supply of pins, but no staples or paper clips.

I suspect the first historic article Mother wrote was a feature about the William Knoch Cigar Store and Factory, which opened in 1883 and flourished until 1931 when the owner died. Mother knew that William's son, Win

Knoch, who had become a U.S. Appeals Court judge, was a source of first-hand information about old-time families in Naperville. Win had co-chaired Naperville's Centennial Celebration in 1931 and could be counted on to provide historic information about the city. As a youngster and teenager, Win had worked in his father's cigar factory and later on Saturdays and afternoons while attending DePaul University Law School.

On the back of an undated "Story of the Week" about three generations of the Drendel family, descendants of Theresa and Xavier Drendel, was Jim Givler's following Town Talk column and part of a *Clarion* masthead dated Feb. 3, 1949. He begins his column:

"'Early Naperville Families' is the subject of a series of articles starting in this issue of The Clarion in The Story of the Week column. As far as possible, the articles will include a genealogy of the family, beginning with the first families' settler."

He went on to explain the *Clarion* was only able to print the Drendel family tree of the first three generations, but members of the sixth generation planned to bring their genealogy up to date in time for a great family reunion the following summer.

Was the series Jim Givler's idea or Mother's? I could find no record of who proposed doing the series, but because of the way her stories usually unfolded and because she was given such free rein on topics, I suspect featuring the early families was Mother's idea. Being the easy-going man he was and also a member of a longtime Naperville family, Jim was pleased to have this kind of feature in his paper, I'm sure. They began to add reader appeal, which had been lacking.

Though not all of the pioneer family stories in the *Clarion* were selected for inclusion in *A View of Historic Naperville*; the Joseph and John Naper story, originally published July 14, 1949, in the *Clarion*, of course, was selected. It has been referred to many times as Naperville has celebrated multiple anniversaries of its 1831 founding since that 1949 date. Mother chose to do that story at that particular time because it was in July, 118 years earlier, that the Naper brothers and their families had arrived at the DuPage River. She had learned of the Napers' arrival date from Richmond and Vallette's 1857 *History of DuPage County*. This was one of the valuable volumes kept in the Martin-Mitchell Museum's maid's room.

This small back room had become a library when the Martin family's home became a museum in 1939. Its contents included many of Naperville's original historical records. How Mother loved that room! There, she found so much inspiration in old records and old newspapers. She was grateful for folks like Mattie Eggerman, who was one of Naperville's first full-time librarians and in effect, also the town's first historian. It was she who preserved many of Naperville's valuable records. Mother also appreciated the efforts of the museum's corresponding-secretary, Walter M. Givler, (Jim Givler's uncle) as well as untold others, who had the foresight to arrange a way to preserve those historic materials in the museum. Bertha Finkbeiner and Ruth Gamertsfelder were among the early-dedicated volunteers to host at the museum on Sunday afternoons from spring into fall. Helen Fraser, who had a background in historic conservation, moved to Naperville in 1971 and became another dedicated volunteer to preserve Naperville's history. She was soon given the half time position of assistant curator and later a full time position in 1977 when the museum opened for more hours and developed further education programs. Many times Mother shared with me how helpful these special friends had been.

If Mother were not at home when I came back from school and I hadn't remembered hearing of her specific plans for the day, I knew she could be found at the museum in that upstairs room, with notebook and papers spread about. If we were having windy weather and I happened to be home as she took off for the museum, she would wear a headscarf to keep the wind out of her ears. (Prone to catching respiratory infections, she thought a headscarf reduced this possibility.) Her writing materials were carried in a colorful tote bag and she wore her sturdy walking shoes. I always smiled whenever I saw her carrying the tote with a "Grapevine" design, which I had given her, in homage to her column of the same name. Because the museum was only open to the public on Sunday afternoons from 2 to 5 p.m., she must have been given a key that allowed her access to the museum's library anytime of day or night. How wonderful that she was so trusted and accommodated!

She was very fortunate that Naperville folk artist, Lester Schrader, gave her permission to use many of his paintings of early Naperville to illustrate her historic articles. Fourteen of these paintings also illustrate *A View of Historic Naperville*. From the 1940s to 1981, three years before he died, Les painted 42 of these folk art paintings, which depict the history of Naperville. Ironically, his last painting, completed for Naperville's Sesquicentennial Celebration in 1981, depicted the first part of Naperville's history – Joseph and John Naper arriving in the area with other families from Ashtabula, Ohio.

Les's research for his paintings was similar to the way Mother researched her stories. He talked with old timers, sought out old photos and studied the landscape where his painted scenes took place. His paintings now form the basis of a permanent exhibit titled, "Brushstrokes of the Past…Naperville's Story," housed in the Pre-Emption House Visitor Center at Naper Settlement in downtown Naperville. There is also a recreation of Les's artist's studio that was located across the street from the museum village.

Mother's June 1950 feature on the Martin-Mitchell Mansion, which is one of the *Clarion* articles included in the book, called into focus how it had become a museum and how generous Caroline Martin Mitchell had been to bequeath her estate to the city. My high school friend, Betty May Smith, and I were two of the early volunteer guides. We noticed that Mother's article precipitated a slight increase in Sunday afternoon visitors. We enjoyed bragging about the wonderful house, and Mr. Givler, the museum host, let us don two of the Victorian dresses we had found in an upstairs closet. We enjoyed being "of the period" for about six Sundays.

Her 1968 *Sun* article, "Bailey Hobson and his House" was one of the articles that featured a Naperville home of distinction as well as an in-depth history of the Hobson family and their mill. She wrote features on both of these themes. She also liked to use her columns to build support for worthwhile charities. She pointed out that the Naperville Garden Club had selected the Hobson House as one of the buildings on their annual tour of homes during the Illinois Sesquicentennial year. One of the reasons she featured the home was most likely that her sister-in-law, Grace Fredenhagen, and Grace's husband, Walter, owned the house, refurbishing it from complete disrepair to one of the most beautiful and historic homes in the area.

As much as she treasured doing research on Naperville's earliest families, homes and businesses, it was her interviews with old timers that gave her the most joy and put "life" into her articles. I remember how animated she would be at the supper table after her interviews with amazing folks such as Truman Myers, former livery driver, postmaster and talented bass singer, as well as pioneering photographer and merchant, Eli Stark. Another great source for her historic stories was Mae Ballou Beckman, local benefactor and philanthropist, whose father made his fortune during the Gold Rush.

Of all the stories she shared, my husband's favorite, is the one Mother gleaned from Augie Germann, the talented Naperville businessman who was born in the "Brew House." The Kroehler Company was at one time the world's largest furniture manufacturer. Its first plant was established in Naperville. Peter Kroehler arranged to bring in many German artisans to get the factory started. Many Napervillle families with German names relate to that endeavor. An observant German entrepeneur by the name of Peter Stenger felt that such a collection of countrymen needed a good beer. He immigrated bringing with him a master brewer and set up the Stenger Brewery. The old limestone building still existed when Dick and I were growing up. Using Naperville's great spring water, the beer was a great success and was becoming popular in the Chicago area, much to the benefit of Herr Stenger. He suggested to his master brewer that if he would marry his daughter that he would inherit the thriving business. The brewer was apparently not attracted to the offer because he fled a thousand miles away to Golden, Colorado and started his own business.

Genevieve, always the professional journalist, called the incumbent president of that brewery to confirm the facts. He did confirm that she had "Grandpa's story." The brewer's name was Adolf Coors.

As she became a writer of increasing note, several local businesses asked her to write their company's history. Naperville National Bank was one of these. There was a separate section of the *Sun* about the bank on its 25th anniversary that was attractively printed with a glossy finish. As she was preparing that story, I'm sure she had some grateful memories. That was the bank, newly opened in 1934, which lent Mother and Dad money to build their Julian Street home. Both of the town's other banks had closed during the Depression and never reopened.

When another local business, Beidelman-Kunsch Funeral Home, thought their family had been in business in Naperville for 120 years, John Kunsch asked Mother to write their history in 1983. The funeral home, along with Oswald's Pharmacy, is one of the oldest continuously operating businesses in Naperville. Because the funeral home's beginnings were based on hearsay, they had asked a secretary, Elizabeth Schmitt, to see what she could find in old newspapers at Nichols Library. She found two articles that stated that the business was started in 1861, not 1863, as they had believed and advertised. They were rather sheepish to admit this mistake, but Mother told them it made little difference at that point and assured them she would still write their story. Following that article, she was supplied with high quality Beidelman-Kunsch ballpoint pens for her writing, which she enjoyed for many years.

When Cock Robin, originally Prince Castle, was 40 years old, Mother wrote that company's story in 1971, which carried many memories for her. While working in the offices of the Naperville Creamery Company, the forerunner of Prince Castle, she met Dad.

Of course, it was a given that she would write the history of the *Naperville Sun* in 1965 when the paper was 30 years old. There was an addendum to that story in 1975 to highlight its amazing development through the years.

No one anticipated how well-received *A View of Historic Naperville* would be. The date of its first publication Nov. 1, 1975, was just in time for the Naperville Heritage Society's Annual Antique Show, Christmas, and our nation's Bicentennial. The Naperville Heritage Society had become the administrators of the Martin-Mitchell Museum and held the antique show as an annual fundraiser. Since it was a "coming out party" for the book, I went to Naperville for the occasion. I found her at the show, dressed in prairie dress at a signing desk, ready to oblige any requests. There was a second printing as early as May 1976 and three more printings by September 1990. Some realtors would present a copy to each of their new homeowners. Corporations that were transferring employees to the Naperville area would send them a copy. Mother told me with pride that Miriam Fry, senior librarian at Nichols Library, had said that *A View of Historic Naperville* was checked out more frequently than any other book on their shelves. When Anderson's Bookstore and the Naper Settlement gift shop had no more books in stock, *A View of Historic Naperville* became a sought after yard-sale purchase. Nichols Library had to declare its volume for library use only. Eventually, the book was reprinted in 2006 in honor of Naperville's 175th anniversary and is back on bookstore shelves. The book also was distributed to Rotarians around the world who visited Naperville during their annual convention.

The impact Mother's articles have had on the community is immeasurable. They have provided a wealth of information about the history of Naperville that, otherwise, would have vanished with the deaths of the longtime residents she interviewed, who would have carried the town's history with them to their graves. A wonderful resource for researchers, genealogists, journalists and those who want to learn more about the history of Naperville, Illinois, the meticulously written and edited book is a tribute to Mother's incredible writing skills and her love of her adopted hometown.

15

Inclusion and Diversity

I think Mother always had an intense interest in people, all kinds of people, as well as a strong sense of social justice. This was a core part of her being and her writing reflected that. Michael Ebner, the charming professor of history emeritus at Lake Forest College in Lake Forest, Ill., commented that her columns not only chronicled Naperville's changes, but they also influenced the changes. It was through her "Sky-lines" and "Grapevine" columns that Naperville met many of its new residents.

In the 1940s when Mother started writing her columns, Naperville had very little diversity in its population. When researching the history of DuPage County, where Naperville is located, it is clear that most of the people who settled in the area were of European descent. Naperville was founded by Joseph Naper, his family and friends who hailed from Ashtabula, Ohio. Previously, their families came from New England, moving west looking for a better life for their families. In the 1840s, immigrants from Germany seeking religious freedom began to settle in the area. It wasn't until the 1960s that a shift in the makeup of Naperville's population began when international corporations such as Amoco and Bell Laboratories and Argonne National Laboratory located large research facilities in the community, which attracted people from all over the world to work at these premier organizations. Up until that time, despite the fact that Naperville was only 30 miles from Chicago and was the home of North Central College, it was a rather insulated community, surrounded by farms. This was the environment that allowed "the beach controversary" to occur that I described in chapter 13. It illustrates how courageous her writing was in that summer of 1954 to try to effect change.

Mother used her column to introduce Naperville's newest residents, who might be viewed as different because of their race or background. One of her columns featured William and Chio Yaginuma, who had come to Naperville in the 1940s seeking work at what was then Edward Sanitarium, which served patients recovering from tuberculosis. The Yaginumas were born in California and had attended college there. William graduated from Davis Agricultural College and Chio attended junior college. Their lives and the lives of countless others were changed when Pearl Harbor was attacked on Dec. 7, 1941.

Because each of their families lived close to military installations in California, they were among the thousands of Japanese-Americans who were relocated to internment camps, ostensibly because they were considered an "invasion threat" to United States security. William and Chio's families were given 48 hours to dispose of and pack up their belongings before they were sent to one of the most infamous camps - Manzanar in Owens Valley, California. In the midst of the hardship and depravation at Manzanar, it was there that William and Chio met and married.

In 1943, they were given permission to leave the camp because there were employment opportunities in the Midwest. The couple came to Naperville to help alleviate an employment shortage at Edward Sanatorium, which became Edward Hospital. Later, Bill worked two other jobs and also worked at a local filling station in Naperville. He became a gasoline attendant at the Clyde C. Netzley dealership.

Even after the U.S. government allowed Japanese-Americans to return to their homes in California, the Yaginumas chose to stay in Naperville. They purchased a home north of the Naperville train station in an area called Park Addition. Unfortunately, William died before he was 60 from a debilitating illness thought to have been precipitated by his grueling work while helping to establish the relocation camps. Chio stayed in Naperville for another 10 years before moving back to California. The Yaginuma family left an indelible mark on Naperville and became woven into the increasingly diverse fabric of the community.

Mother celebrated the accomplishments of another longtime community member and successful business owner, Sam Chan of Sam Lung Laundry. Lung was the Chinese word for laundry. For three years, Sam was tutored in reading and writing by local resident, Martha Koehler, so he could take the test to become a U.S. citizen. In 1949, he passed the citizenship test, and at the federal building in Chicago, pledged allegiance to his new country.

The following year, he chose local tax consultant, Gerald Myers, to help prepare his taxes. When Sam found out he was due a refund, he wanted to revise the return so he could pay taxes to his new country!

Mother always loved writing about North Central College and the Evangelical Theological Seminary. When she wanted to feature international students from either institution, they would come to our house to be interviewed in the living room. I'm sure they also enjoyed being treated to Mother's famous baked goods, such as her caramel pecan rolls, doughnuts or pecan butter cookies. One of her earliest articles, dated Feb. 10, 1949, is about three seminary students, Isaac Willems, who had been a missionary in Venezuela; Howard Box who was a Canadian; and Joseph Ma, a Christian minister who had served in war-torn China. They shared their stories with Mother, who would enthusiastically write about their contributions, in turn sharing them with the Naperville community.

As Mother's columns gained a following, readers would often be eager to tell her about interesting new residents. This helped her to learn about the Pribel family, which in turn became an article titled, "From Austria to Naperville – From Heartbreak to Joy," published Sept. 6, 1951, in the *Naperville Clarion.*

Ludwig Pribel was born in the United States, but through a series of circumstances, returned to his country of origin, Austria. When his mother died in childbirth and his father had been conscripted into the Austrian army because World War I began, Ludwig was adopted by his aunt and uncle, the Heindrichs. When the Heindrichs hit upon hard times here in the U.S., they took their nephew with them to the family farm in Austria. By the early 1930s, the part of Austria where they lived became part of Romania. After Ludwig's uncle died in 1935, the family continued to live there. Ludwig married Amalia in 1938, but in two years, war broke out in their country and the couple and his aunt fled to Salzburg, Austria, to escape Communist troops that had invaded Romania.

For five years, they lived in a refugee camp with little or no conveniences, storing coal to heat their meager dwelling under their beds. Because Ludwig was an American citizen, he was able to drive trucks for U.S. troops stationed in that city. Life in the refugee camp was anything but normal, but Ludwig and his wife had two children, Aricka and Herbert. When Germany surrendered in 1945, because of Ludwig's American citizenship, he was able to come to Naperville where an uncle lived. The family was torn apart as he was only able to bring his daughter, Aricka, with him. The rest of his family was left behind. After months of waiting, the remaining family members were granted visas and were reunited in their new hometown of Naperville. I'm sure there were many stories like this throughout the country after World War II, but Mother made it locally vivid.

Another facility that attracted an international employee base was Argonne National Laboratory in nearby Lemont, Ill. One Naperville resident, who had the distinction of being part of a team that developed the first computer, was Dr. Jeffrey Chu. Mother's "Story of the Week" published Oct. 18, 1951, in the *Naperville Clarion* had the unusual headline of "Naperville Scientist works on 'Mechanical Brains.'" Evidently, in 1951, "mechanical brain" was better understood than the word "computer." Her story highlighted the fact that a Naperville resident was working on one of the nation's newest inventions of which there were less than half a dozen in existence. While most of the computers were so large that they filled an entire gymnasium, Dr. Chu was proud of the fact that the two they were building at Argonne only took up the space of an ordinary room. She noted how the young scientist, "speaks of them as easily as if they were a household gadget."

The Chus were among the earliest Argonne families to move to Naperville. Dr. Chu was named senior scientist at Argonne in 1949, and his family moved to Naperville in 1950. Recognizing that someone of such caliber would be an asset to the educational system, Ralph Beebe, superintendent of Naperville schools, invited him and other respected scientists to participate in the school district's planning groups and curriculum building. The final sentence in Mother's column was printed in bold and read, "Naperville is indeed fortunate that such an outstanding scientist and his family should choose our town in which to live."

Naperville's population did indeed become more diverse through the years. Mother's "Grapevine" column, published Dec. 1, 1977, described Marian Schlueter's fourth-grade class at Mill Street Elementary School in Naperville. Because nine different countries were represented in this class, Marian encouraged the children to talk about their backgrounds and to bring artifacts of their heritage for "show and tell." On a large map of the world, she flagged the countries represented. She also planned to enlist the parents to share more of their cultural heritage with the class.

Mother also wrote about the American Association of University Women's Culture-Sharing Group. Sharon Shou, who was part of the group and told Mother about its existence, realized that many of Naperville's newest residents were isolated and did not know how to connect with other community members. The monthly Culture-Sharing Group meetings, held in AAUW members' homes, provided the perfect venue to break through cultural barriers, create lasting friendships, and to sample cuisine from other countries.

As the population grew in Naperville, Mother's columns celebrated the cultural diversity that came with this growth. From Muslim and Hindu groups to the establishment of the new Congregation Beth Shalom synagogue or a new Chinese Lutheran Church, she noted that each accomplishment was wonderful for Naperville. She often described how Naperville found ways to welcome the new residents, such as the establishment of Chinese schools, where children were taught the language. She also described Naperville Community School District 203's English as a Second Language program where at one time 82 students from 27 nations were enrolled.

Hardly a month went by without one of Mother's columns featuring a new family, originally from a different country, which had chosen to live in Naperville. The columns celebrated the enrichment of the community and encouraged others to live here, too.

{ 16 }
Genevieve's Favorite Subjects

If Naperville residents faithfully read either the *Sky-Lines* or *Grapevine* columns in their weekly issues of *The Naperville Sun* for a year, they would soon realize that Mother had some favorite subjects. There must have been some readers who thought, "Oh, here she goes again," but more would have wondered how she kept coming up with so many interesting stories about the same subjects. She had a passionate interest in Naperville's people and causes, and she wanted to spread the word about them. The subjects she enjoyed writing about most were historic in nature, but other subjects also reflected her many passions.

Four of the chapters in *A View of Historic Naperville* featured Naperville's North Central College, including "Yesterday's Mansion, Bolton Hall," "College Celebrates

Centennial In 1961," "*Chronicle* Reflects Life on Campus" and "Fifty-Year Graduates Recall Student Days."

If alert readers hadn't noticed already, in her Dec. 12, 1984, *Grapevine* column, she finally admitted that she had a special interest in the school since North Central was her alma mater. At that time, her association with the college spanned 60 years from the day she first enrolled as a freshman in 1924. The subject of this 1984 *Grapevine* column was the college's Annual Report, not usually a topic of high interest unless one is a member of the Board of Trustees. However, under Mother's gifted touch, she made it fascinating.

Her "then and now" comparisons were surprising as she listed the changes at the college over time. In 1924, all of the trustees were men and most were preachers, affiliated with the Evangelical Church, the denomination that had established the college. One of the perks the church offered was free tuition for 25 years to the descendants of anyone who contributed $100. My husband, Richard Moy, related that his maternal great-grandfather mortgaged the farm in order to contribute to the college's establishment. True to its origins, the college was very conservative — no dancing, no card playing, no smoking and, of course, no drinking. Daily attendance at chapel was required. Most of the student body was white, Anglo-Saxon and Protestant.

By 1984, Mother reported five of the 41 trustees were women. Others were business executives, physicians, lawyers, bankers and educators and two were church bishops. Compared to 1924, the college's curriculum was broader and the substantial growth in the budget and committed gifts was impressive. What was most impressive was how Mother took the college's "nuts and bolts" Annual Report and turned it into a feature in which the message was "Look at this gem we have in Naperville!"

Two of Mother's *Clarion* articles that my Grandmother Brayton clipped and pinned around 1948-1949 were indicative of those particular years in North Central's history. One column was about World War II veterans living in barracks on campus, and the other was about Minnie Tarnoski who ran a boarding club for North Central students. (These were private homes where home cooked meals were served regularly to a group of students who had rented sleeping rooms in another home.)

"Our Married Veterans Attend College" was an article about 21 ex-GI families and chronicled life in the campus barracks housing that had been built for them on Fort Hill. She noted the average age of the couples was 25 and most had one child. Three families had two children. In addition to the former GIs attending college, several of the wives also took courses. Living on campus was not inexpensive and couples paid 22 percent of their income for rent, plus their own fuel. If a veteran had one or more children, he received $120 a month from the government, but with that meager sum, it was imperative that these veterans seek supplementary income. Kroehler Manufacturing Company, the furniture manufacturer located near the college, employed half of them. Because the barracks were constructed in a similar style, to avoid confusion, each couple worked out different color schemes and window treatments, putting their own personalities into the meagerly furnished quarters.

Mother's other feature was tribute to Minnie Tarnoski who was chief cook in the college dining halls for 29 years. Prior to being employed at the college, she ran a student boarding club in her home, where she had college boys as roomers for 45 years. Mother remembered when she was a student that Mrs. Tarnoski was running a boarding club as far back as the 1920s. After Mrs. Tarnoski's husband, Albin, was burned and blinded in a terrible explosion at his job, she, her husband and their son moved to Naperville. Because of her husband's disability, Mrs. Tarnoski had to find a way to make a living and maintain a home for her family. They chose to rent a home, and as a means of generating a steady source of income, they rented the upstairs of their home to college boys. Fortunately, she never lacked for roomers. One young man, Ben Zinders, had the all-time record of living with the family for 11 years. He attended the college's academy first, to obtain his high school diploma, went on to receive his college degree and then graduated from the seminary. At one point, she had as many as 36 people at her home for whom she cooked meals three times a day.

During World War I, college authorities asked her to board part of the ROTC (Reserve Officer Training Corp) military group on campus until facilities in Old Main could be completed. Later, she took over the dining hall in Old Main where during some semesters she fed as many as 280 a day. When the Kaufman Hall dormitory was built, she was chosen to preside over its kitchen.

She described the biggest thrill of her life that came several years before she retired. In an interview with Mother, she said, "President Edward Rall telephoned me one day and said, 'Mrs. Tarnoski, do you have a nice dress?' Knowing he could always take a joke, she asked, 'Why, do you want to buy me one?' He replied, 'No, but tomorrow is commencement and it is your turn to graduate. Put on your nicest dress because you'll be up on the platform.'"

One of the hardest working employees at North Central was to be recognized for her 25 years of service to the college, just as they would honor professors who served a similar number of years. When she was called to the platform, she received the most applause ever heard in Pfeiffer Hall up to that time. Because of her longtime association with the college and the community, many of her former roomers and boarders were among the parents of the graduates. There was so much cheering and hollering that Dr. Rall became so excited that he forgot, at the time, to present her with the $25 gift, which he had in his pocket. Before she retired, it was estimated she had fed more than 5,000 students.

Of course, time marches on, and changes continued to occur at the college. The barracks had disappeared by 1951 and the last time there was a listing for a dining club was in the 1959-60 campus directory of which the Southeastern Club was the last survivor. But the kindness of Minnie Tarnoski and her contributions was legendary.

In addition to North Central College, Naperville organizations that could count on Mother for support included Little Friends School and the Naperville Heritage Society. Since their inception in the 1960s, both have become a significant part of the Naperville community. Each group credits her writing as making a great difference in their development, and Mother was keenly aware that her articles played a major role in the early success of these two groups. Through the years, the groups came to count on her for applause for their accomplishments or to announce an upcoming event. Watching them grow gave Mother real satisfaction.

In 1981, Mother was invited to attend the Christmas program at Little Friends School. "Along with the smiles on my face there was a lump in my throat and tears in my eyes," she wrote. Watching this demonstration of achievement, she remembered how she became involved with Little Friends. She recalled in a column, "I kept remembering a certain morning in the fall of 1964, when four ladies came to my home to tell me of their hopes and plans for starting a class for severely mentally retarded children — children for whom there was no place in the public schools' special education programs. They asked my help in presenting their plan to readers of the *Sun*. One of those four ladies was Dottie Krejci who was to be the teacher of the proposed class three afternoons a week."

The four women evidently found it a memorable visit, not only because Genevieve was so responsive, but because she greeted them at the door wearing a flour-covered apron and served them her freshly made doughnuts. Since that significant visit, Dottie was with Little Friends every step of the way, as she watched it grow from that first little class of five students to an agency serving children with various emotional and behavioral problems, mentally handicapped babies and mentally challenged adults.

In less than 20 years, the agency had many full-time programs, several with live-in situations, and occupied all of the facilities of North Central's former Kroehler campus, named for the majestic home that was furniture manufacturer Peter Kroehler's family mansion. In addition to the Naperville campus, there was a sheltered workshop in a factory building in Downers Grove; a program for babies in St. John's United Church of Christ; a group home for autistic children in Wheaton; and several apartments where graduates lived with support staff. When Mother wrote about Little Friends in 1981, there were over 370 enrolled in various programs. Just at Little Friends School alone, there were 114 pupils and 61 staff persons. The agency received funds from the Department of Mental health and some from Naperville's Community Fund, an organization which helped fund not-for-profit groups. Another funding source was the annual Little Friends Auction, which not only generated revenue, but also a great deal of enthusiastic support from the community for this special agency. No wonder I frequently heard euphoric reports about this unique place in our weekly phone calls!

The Naperville Heritage Society also credits Genevieve with a role influencing its development. In 1969, St. John's Episcopal Church was threatened with demolition. A group of concerned citizens read in Genevieve's *Grapevine* column of the impending historic crisis and sent out a call to action. The 1864 Gothic Revival church was in the way of future development at the site, which was located near North Central, and would need to be moved in order to save it. Led by Jane Sindt, the Heritage Society was organized in February 1969 with the goal to save this historic church. In a plea for assistance voiced in Mother's column, they invited others to join with them to raise enough funds. In less than a year, they raised $20,000 to move the church across town to city-owned property near the Martin-Mitchell Museum.

Throughout the harrowing first months of their existence, as the Heritage Society struggled to raise the money to save the church, Mother agreed to give them any publicity they needed for fundraising. She wrote about the church's significance and about the volunteers known as the Weed Ladies, who collected weeds from the highways and byways of empty lots and fields to create attractive bouquets and arrangement that they sold at the Antiques Show in their popular Country Store. She encouraged readers to join the Heritage Society and to support the fledgling efforts at preservation that began with saving the church and then continued to include many other buildings.

Thanks in part to Mother's support, the church was saved and was completely renovated, becoming known as Century Memorial Chapel. Through the years, many of her *Sun* features were about other rescued buildings including the Murray House, the Paw Paw Post Office, the Daniels House and Halfway House, named because it marked the halfway point between Naprville and Aurora. The historic homes formed the core of the historic village known as Naper Settlement. She wrote about the tireless volunteers who worked on the restorations or the local companies and unions that donated labor and materials. The annual Antiques Show, which was the Heritage Society's major fundraiser, became known as one of the best in the Chicago area.

Also she wasn't averse to assuming the role of trading post. "Anyone have a spare deacon's bench?" was the kind of request she'd put in her *Grapevine* column when there was a special need at the Settlement. In 1982, volunteers were readying a portion of the chapel's basement as a bride's room. It already had an impressive floor-to-ceiling mirror and lovely window treatments, but a deacon's bench would complete the furnishings. She also asked for a much-needed dehumidifier to dry up the damp floor. Generous residents would always come to the rescue. She loved her role of connecting people with needs to people with the needed resources.

Another organization that appreciated this connecting was the Community Chorus. A group of singers was hoping to organize a local group. Mother was willing to announce their plans in her *Grapevine* column, which had such positive results that she was made an honorary member of the chorus.

The Summer Place Theatre started out in a tent on Fort Hill on the campus of North Central College, and she was an immediate booster for it. I think it brought back memories of when she was in dramatics in college and briefly in an amateur group early in her marriage. She had great respect for two of the founders, Don Jamison and Donald Shanower, who had been associated with North Central. Every season she announced the coming attractions. If there were improvements in the setting, Mother noted those, too. She could be counted on for an honest review of the performances from each season's offerings, but she always found something good to say about what she saw even if she had criticism.

There were a few individuals who were so interesting that she often wrote about them. Of all of these Naperville notables, I think Harold Henning topped the list. Hal was an outstanding swimmer who had graduated from North Central and was slated to go to the Tokyo Olympics when World War II intervened. He never realized his dream of swimming in the Olympics, but served on many of the International Olympic Games committees over the years and became president of FINA, the International Swimming Federation. He traveled to all the Olympic games, planning meetings and International Swimming Championship Meets. He and his wife, Jean Oliver Henning, the daughter of one of Mother's beloved North Central professors, provided interesting behind-the-scenes stories about these adventures and fodder for her columns. When the Hennings were attending the 1982 World Swimming Championships in Guayaquil, Ecuador, they connected with Antonio Cohen, an Ecuadorian foreign exchange student, who had attended Naperville North High School the previous year. This was the kind of serendipitous event that Mother loved to write about in her *Grapevine* column. Hal seemed to appreciate what she wrote, for when he returned from each Olympics he would give her a small remembrance from his travels. I inherited one item he brought her, which is an olive wood carving of a camel train and is an important part of our Christmas Nativity scene every year.

Another successful businessman and "hometown boy" that Mother loved to write about was Al Rubin. He served on more community boards and committees than one could count. Al's father moved to Naperville in the 1930's, and they were the first Jewish family to arrive in the community. Al started the Rafter House Restaurant in Naperville, and then went on to become one of the Midwest's top foodservice providers. Mother chronicled the growth of his business and wrote a two-issue feature about his trip to China in 1980 when that country was just starting to be open for tourism. Al credited the picture in the geography book used in Miss Betlach's fourth grade class at Naper School with whetting his appetite for his China trip. His story was unique, because in addition to the typical tourist experiences, he vividly described the different kinds of foods he was served. Before Al left, Mother learned that his trip included a stop in Okinawa where her grandson, Guy Bernardin, was stationed with the U.S. Air Force. As a testament to their friendship, Al connected with Guy and they had lunch together.

At Mother's memorial service, Al recounted how he thought she had legitimatized his marriage. He and his wife, Naomi, had been married in northern Michigan, but it wasn't until several weeks after the wedding that the announcement was given to the *Sun* for publication. Because of the length of time from their marriage to when the announcement was going to be published, the *Sun* told Al that it was old news and wouldn't print it. Al said that folks were wondering if they were living in sin, since there had been nothing in the paper about their wedding. He called Mother, who quickly wrote about the marriage and the small town busybodies stopped their gossiping.

In 1986, Mother acknowledged that she had written more about Dr. Gus Constantine than any other North Central faculty member. In 1960, he came with his family to head up North Central's Department of Education. Through the years, his expertise took him to several states and foreign countries and he was selected to go to Russia with a group of educators before that Communist country allowed Western tourists. Dr. Constantine was a fascinating individual and Mother wrote about many of his experiences. In his 26-year career at North Central, he was responsible for the certifications of more than 2,000 teachers.

I have to selfishly acknowledge that two of her favorite subjects were my husband, Dick, and, yes, me. Dick was newsworthy because he was the founding dean of the Southern Illinois University School of Medicine. She loved writing about the awards he received and his medical education trip to Africa. Occasionally, Naperville readers read about one of my achievements, but too often it was about my health, a fractured skull when I was thrown from a horse or my recovery from ovarian cancer and its complications. It was a bit embarrassing, but it wasn't unusual for me to meet someone who had lived in Naperville and they would say, "Oh, I've read about you!"

There was one of my activities that I was especially pleased she wrote about — our 1977 Christmas dinner. I surprised Daddy and her by serving the same menu for Christmas dinner that my grandmother had served sixty years earlier in Idaho in 1917. The year 1977 was when my folks moved from 417 S. Julian St. to The Holmstad retirement center in Batavia. While cleaning out the attic, we found a detailed letter Grandma Brayton had written to cousins in Oak Park. It included the menu, the toasts, those present and much more. I used the same china that had been used in 1917. I had been able to sneak Mother's Naperville Heritage Society costume out of her closet so we women could be in an appropriate costume. Dandelion wine was the most difficult item to obtain, but two wine hobbyists traded me the wine for sugar. Mother later sent me a long list of readers who commented on the article.

I think the extent of her readership is best illustrated when she would request something of readers. She learned a foster home was needed for one young boy with special circumstances. Several families answered that request, and the Illinois Department of Children and Family Services selected one family and placed the boy with them. In her column, she thanked her readers and those who had volunteered to help.

She wrote about the need for host families for a summer program that included both Protestant and Catholic children from Ireland. Seven families volunteered prior to her request, and 34 responded after her column was published. She gave a follow-up thank you for that response, too.

One time she wrote that the book, *Head Hunting in the Solomon Islands*, had been sold at the yard sale she and Dad held, and now, he wanted to read it again. If one of her readers had bought it, could they buy it back? One reader brought it to them, and Dad gave him a quarter, the price the buyer paid for it six months earlier.

She was so proud of so much in Naperville: the Riverwalk, Nichols Library, Naperville's churches, unique giving organizations such as FISH, the novel person to person helping service. She wrote a long *Grapevine* piece on the encouraging support for the planned Independent Living Center. She was so proud of Martin Manor, Naperville's first housing project for the elderly, which became Martin Avenue Apartments.

She wrote about special people like Charlotte Marous, who overcame physical challenges and became a successful businesswoman, selling flowering plants in her "Wee Flower Shop," and Valerian Deodiuc, the custodian at the YMCA for more 30 years. She also advocated the establishment of a Naperville Community Chest. To track volunteer hours and funding, she herself started keeping track of all the organizations that asked for money in one year and wrote a strong plea for what so many of the neighboring towns had found effective. This was the precursor to the Naperville United Way.

She wrote a strong column of outrage when she learned that the Nichols Library Board of Directors was considering changing the name to Naperville Library. Former North Central College Professor James Nichols, turned successful publisher, had donated funds to establish the library, and she believed it would be a large insult to remove that name. In the end, Nichols Library remained the name of the main branch, while the umbrella organization is called the Naperville Public Library, which is the No. 1 library for a city of Naperville's size in the nation. Eventually, two additional branches were established to serve the growing Naperville population – the Naper Boulevard branch and the 95th Street branch.

In going through the huge box of rescued columns found by chance in the offices of the *Naperville Sun*, I was especially impressed with the great number of tributes she wrote in over 40 years. Some of them were written after the individuals had died, such as the one she wrote for Robert Van Adestine and Walter Hoel, both of whom had long, dedicated careers at Naperville High School. Mr. Hoel was an amazing senior English teacher. Those of us Naperville High School graduates who keep in touch still talk about his rendition of the drunken gatekeeper in Shakespeare's *Macbeth*. Mr. Van Adestine was the long-serving principal. Close friends, they died just over a year apart and are buried in side-by-side family plots in Naperville Cemetery.

She congratulated poet, Glenna Holloway, on her awards. She believed Helen Fraser turned the Martin Mitchell Museum into more than a museum, but also an educational resource available for the entire community. She was amazed at how Roy Grundy had pursued his interest in knowing more about Stephen Scott, a Naperville pioneer, and learned much more than Naperville records had first indicated. She often was the first person to give an "attaboy" or "attagirl" for a special achievement. She might also be the last to write a poignant comment on the community's loss when a contributing citizen had died.

But of all the organizations in Naperville, Mother wrote more articles about North Central College than any other subject. Faculty accomplishments always made a good story, as did its students, particularly the foreign students. Early in 1995, North Central College President Harold Wilde visited Japan where he met with Japanese alumni, who had attended North Central. While visiting these former students, he learned of Mother's death. Many told President Wilde that they still had the clippings from the *Naperville Sun* articles that Genevieve Towsley had written about them. Certainly their reaction was a testimony to the power of the press and Mother's positive influence on the Naperville community. The love for her alma mater always showed through in the many articles and columns she wrote about North Central College.

❋ 17 ❋
Genevieve's Faith and Her Church

Church always played a big part in Mother's life. In her Idaho childhood story, she told of the family attending services held in the Canyonside School where the Rev. Robert Lloyd Roberts ministered to a Presbyterian congregation. Rev. Roberts also served two other churches in Jerome and Arcadia and was frequently invited to have Sunday meals with the Braytons before going on to his next church. Receiving inspiration from the man whom the family called an "ardent young preacher" and their close relationship with him had an impact on Mother her entire life.

She remembered that his living a Christian faith as well as voicing it was genuinely appealing. Those who knew Mother could easily describe her faith in the same manner. Her Christian beliefs were strong at a young age. By the time she was 13, she was teaching Sunday school, picking up some of her pupils in the horse and buggy she drove the three miles from her home to Canyonside School where both church services and Sunday school were held.

Several years later, when the family moved back to Oak Park, she first learned about North Western College from her Sunday school teacher. While in college, she joined First Evangelical Church, the present Community United Methodist Church. Despite her early leaning toward that church, evidently the Congregational form of church organization was more pleasing to her and Dad. The Rev. Earl Collins, pastor at First Congregational, married them in a home wedding June 23, 1929, and they both joined the church a few months later on Oct. 13.

Mother, missing the involvement she had at her Idaho church and wanting to live her Christian faith, immediately became an assistant Boy Scout leader to the troop that met at First Congregational. Her affiliation with the church that began with her marriage would have a far deeper impact. As a member of the congregation, she volunteered to write the church's history, long before she ever entertained the idea of being a journalist. She was a young mother with an infant, but she fitted the extensive project into her busy schedule.

The year was 1933 when she wrote the 100-year history of the congregation and served on the Celebration Committee. The Gothic stone church located on Benton Avenue and Center Street was the first church founded in DuPage County and the oldest Congregational church in Northern Illinois. In the amazingly detailed history she compiled, she included this account about then-Sunday school Superintendent Deacon Knickerbocker, which was told at the church's 50th anniversary celebration in 1883.

"Deacon Knickerbocker is said to have carried the school library to and from church in a big red bandana handkerchief. Here is the story. It so happened that Dick Sweet, who was then not as pious as the Deacon, carried his dinner with him to work in a bandana something like the Deacon's. One Sunday Dick had started hunting and had his dinner with him in his handkerchief. He stopped at the saloon and the boys stole the dinner and hid it. He had hunted for it until he was a little impatient, when along came the good Deacon with his Sunday school library in his handkerchief. One of the boys told Dick there was a man with his dinner going down the road. Dick looked and was convinced that this was true. He called out to the deacon to bring back that dinner; but, of course, a Sunday school superintendent could not stop or take any notice of a crowd of loafers about a saloon, and he trudged toward home. Sweet was pretty mad by this time and a little reckless. He called out again, and added that if the dinner was not brought back he would shoot. A soldier of the Lord does not fear threats from sinners, and the Deacon walked bravely on, looking neither to the right nor the left, until there was a crack of a gun and the buckshot flying around him. It so happened that Sweet had taken just enough at the bar to twist his eye a little, and his aim was not good. The Deacon was not hit, but he stopped, and the boys explained and got the missing dinner. Sweet apologized and each went his way."

By 1963, Mother had been a journalist for many years and was an old hand at writing histories. At that time, she wrote an updated history for the church's 130th anniversary. She concluded that history quoting founding Pastor Jeremiah Porter's visionary words, "the mustard seed will become a great tree, so that multitudes shall rest under its delightful shade." History proved him right.

Congregation member, Priscilla Grundy, wrote the 1983 history, but Mother was asked to give an overview of the church's 150-year history at a festive banquet given at what is now the Holiday Inn Select. She and Dad were living in the Holmstad retirement center by then, and she was pleased that the planning committee still wanted her input at the celebration.

I smiled when I read her notes for her speech at that event. In one of our weekly phone conversations, she told me she'd been asked to speak, how pleased she was to have been asked, and then she told me what she had in mind. Apparently, my reaction to her plans was not what she expected, and she described this for the audience:

"Later when I told our daughter, Caryl, about the celebration and what I planned to say, she said, 'Oh, Mother, after those folks have had a cocktail or two and a big dinner, they're not going to want to listen to a lot of history; especially if they're planning to dance afterwards!' Well, that was pretty deflating! I changed my plans then and decided not to talk about each of the pastorates of the 33 pastors that have served this church. Instead, I'll tell just some of the highlights and low lights."

I think the audience was probably relieved that they would only hear a condensed version of the 150-year achievements that evening.

A major crisis in the life of the church that she described took place in the 1950s. The congregation was split over the decision whether or not to merge with the Evangelical and Reformed denominations to become part of the United Church of Christ. About 60 percent of the church

150th Anniversary- First Congregational Church

favored joining in the merger, but a 75 percent vote was required. For over 10 years, the church was at an impasse. As the limbo continued, harsh words were exchanged on both sides. Finally, 120 people withdrew to form the Naperville Congregational Church.

This was a very sad time not only for Mother, but for the entire congregation. Longtime friends were among those choosing to leave for the new church, but Mother felt strongly that the newly united denomination was where she belonged. At times, our conversations about the situation were somewhat tearful. When Senior Pastor Wayne Myers left to accept a position in California, Associate Pastor Stanley Cox was named the senior minister. She thought Cox did a remarkable job of healing the wounds of the separation and bringing the remaining congregation together as a united group, but soon he accepted a pastorate in Canada, his native land,. Finally, in 1969, they had a successful vote to join with the United Church of Christ. For nearly a year, they proved they could still be a church without a full-time pastor.

A long and deliberate search began to find a new pastor. Members of the search committee reviewed resumés and visited churches to listen to sermons and interviews, eventually agreeing on several likely candidates. When they were on the brink of making a recommendation, they received another resumé Mother acknowledged that she protested, saying, "We can't keep considering more and more. We owe it to the congregation to bring them a candidate."

But Julia Christopherson, a retired missionary, had been reading the new resume and spoke up saying, "We can't pass this man up. I've seen him operate at an association meeting. He would be great."

That man was Keith Torney. He declared in his interview that he preached a joyous gospel. After he was hired, Mother said that he was joyous in his Naperville ministry and opened up the congregation to celebrate each other. By the time the new pastor was hired in 1983, she had known nine pastors at First Congregational, but felt there never had been such love and concern as there was with Keith. Dad, who was in his 70s, started going to church again for the first time in 30 years because he said, "He's the only preacher I ever knew that I can be myself with."

Mother had always been a close friend of each of the ministers, corresponding with them for years after they had moved on, but with Keith, the relationship was special. She said that he was the closest person to being a son she ever had.

Minutes of the church meetings indicate that Mother served on many committees through the years. I learned that early in their marriage, Dad served on the music committee. At that time, they both enjoyed the monthly gatherings of a social group for young church couples called the 3F Club, which stood for food, fun and fellowship.

Living her faith was perhaps best shown during the mid 1940's when she was the church's Sunday school director. I remember her planning lessons and arranging for the general opening sessions the evenings before, which must have taken a great deal of organization.

What I remember most about those years was that if we wanted a ride to church, we had to be ready when she left because she had to be sure services started on time. Invariably, my sister, Marian, or I would be running late. We dashed out the front door with ribbons and belts flying to be in time for her to stop by the front steps for us as she backed out of the drive. We would still be hooking belts and tying shoes in the car, but we always managed to be put together by the time we finished the two-mile drive to church each Sunday morning.

As she became a more senior church member, the pastors would seek her advice and suggestions. Sometimes it was for a personal reason, sometimes for her ideas on how to make things happen. In the early 1970s, some churches sponsored families that were refugees from the Vietnam War. Pastor Keith wanted to move ahead quickly to sponsor a family. He called Mother to tell her that a few of mission committee members were in favor of doing this, but he wanted to call the sponsoring organization without the final approval of the congregation. She was quite emphatic in her response that she felt it was unwise to proceed that way. To insure the success of adopting a family, she felt the congregation needed to feel it was part of the decision.

Evidence of Mother's wisdom was apparent when the church said an affectionate goodbye to its adopted family after being part of the Naperville congregation and community for five years. The family was moving to California so the father of the family could take the courses he needed to practice law in this country. Keith gave a loving farewell from the pulpit saying how much the members of the congregation had been enriched by their presence. The children had such a good experience they were wearing tee shirts saying, "Naperville Friends Forever."

Through the years, we had very few conversations about religion because Mother taught us faith by example. Every night without fail, a blessing was said before the evening meal. This was the short prayer we memorized: "For this and all thy gifts of love we give thee thanks and praise;

Look down our Father from above and guide us all our days. Amen." We also had brief bedtime prayers when we thanked God for our mother and father and asked for help in being good.

In her March 2, 1978, *Grapevine* column she expressed her thoughts on prayer in a way I had never heard her speak before. She was commenting on the classic prayer repeated by millions of children, "Now I lay me down to sleep; I pray the Lord my soul to keep. If I should die before I wake, I pray the Lord my soul to take." That prayer caused her to ask her own mother a probing question at a young age. One evening after she had finished saying the classic prayer, she asked, "Mamma, what is my soul?" Her mother looked very surprised and after a couple of minutes replied, "Your soul is the real 'you.' It makes you different from your sister, or your friend Eleanor." That answer satisfied her for the time being.

She acknowledged that even in her 70s, if she were tossing from sleeplessness, she would catch herself saying it involuntarily. Yet, as she analyzed it, she found it most inappropriate for little children and thought the prayer spoke in terms beyond a child's conception. She commented that from her vantage point in life at that time, there were much healthier prayers which children should be taught that didn't need to be so formal.

She remembered several years earlier when she was caring for her grandson, Eric, she had listened to his spontaneous prayer that went, "Dear God, thank you for a happy day. Bless mommy and daddy and Philip (his brother) and make me a good boy. Amen." She thought those few simple statements contained all the attributes of a worthy prayer

—praise of thankfulness to God, concern for others and a desire to follow God's will.

In light of these thoughts and experiences, she asked her friend, Frank Keith, to compose a simple prayer that parents might teach their children. He gave her this lovely verse: "Dear Lord, I thank you for this day; In which no harm has come my way; Now as I sleep, dear Lord above; Enfold me in your arms of love, Amen."

These words captured in a prayer reflected her faith simply and beautifully.

⁂ 18 ⁂
Retirement: A New Beginning

Just after *A View of Historic Naperville* was published in 1975, Dad was beginning to have physical problems. Typically, these seemed coincidental at first. His brief black outs or his stumbling were thought to be of no real consequence and just a sign of aging. These occasional episodes were infrequent enough that in February 1977 when they had lived at 417 S. Julian St. for 40 years, they celebrated by having the entire interior of the seven-room home painted. Mother wrote about the occasion in her *Grapevine* column stating, "I don't want to live anywhere else." Then Dad began to have more obvious mobility problems, particularly climbing stairs. Mother soon had to admit they had a problem because their bedroom was upstairs, as was their full bathroom.

Always a problem solver, she considered several options rather quietly to herself. Should they try to put their bedroom downstairs and eliminate the dining room? She wasn't ready to do that because she still did too much entertaining, casual as it was, with her job at the *Sun*. Should they try to accommodate a live-in caregiver? That seemed extreme for the situation. What about her own mobility issues? Her knees were becoming more arthritic and were giving her a great deal of pain with any significant activity. She often used a cane, and Dad, who relied on a cane to walk, could go nowhere without one. Reluctantly, she raised the issue with him.

Together, it was agreed they needed to move to a retirement center and looked for one that offered continuous care — from relative independence to skilled nursing care and something without stairs. Where to begin? At the time, Naperville had no options that met their requirements. They began driving to nearby communities to visit retirement complexes. Some appeared as possible options until they learned that continuing care in a nursing home facility would not be available. Between the visits to Wheaton or Downers Grove or Aurora, Mother continued writing her usual columns. She was very slow to reach the decision that she would probably have to retire. It became obvious they would no longer be able to live in Naperville, her beloved hometown, which was the setting for most of what she wrote. Its citizens were her readers and the source for her news.

At one of the spring meetings of their dearly loved Naperville Book Club they learned about a new retirement center going up 15 miles away in Batavia that was called the Holmstad. The new center was a Covenant Community, one of the ministries of the Covenant Church, founded by Swedish immigrants. Their Book Club friends, Joe and Gunvar Stoos, were seriously considering moving there. The first units were already built in groups of four small condominium-like structures called "fourplexes." Beyond the reasonable financial requirements, at least one of the persons who planned to live there had to be 50 years old. They also had to be able to leave the building under their own power in an emergency. Besides being an attractive facility, there were plans for a continuing nursing care center. They felt that the Holmstad might be an acceptable solution for their mounting housing needs. Mother and Dad asked that my sister, Marian, and I, and our families come to see the model unit of the Holmstad. If we concurred, they were ready to sign a contract. Marian and her family came from St. Louis and we drove up from downstate Springfield. We all saw the unit and agreed with their decision, so plans were made to move into that model by Sept. 1.

Arrangements for the move meant leaving 40 years of memories connected to their home at 417 S. Julian St. The news of their impending move was carried in her *Grapevine* column. Sadly, in that same issue was the ad listing the house for sale. It only took about a month to receive a satisfactory bid. The house that had been built during the Depression for less than $10,000 was now selling for $70,000 in 1977.

My spring semester of teaching ended, and I went to Naperville to help clean out the attic. I found myself nostalgically wishing I were in a situation where I could be planning to live there. There were a number of families interested in the property, and I was there when the realtor brought my parents the bid that they accepted. The new owners were a scientist at Argonne National Laboratories and his wife, who was a nurse. They had two young boys about the ages as mine. It seemed like a family similar to ours would be living there, so I felt that special house would continue to be loved in the way I loved it.

I'm sure others have had similar experiences when they clear out a home with many memories attached. Cleaning the attic was gut-wrenching. There were tears as well as laughter as Mother and I worked together deciding what to save, what to donate and what to discard. During the process, there were two precious finds. One was a package of ink-faded letters that my great grandmother, Lydia Palmer Brayton, had written to my grandfather who had left Indiana to work in Chicago. If she hadn't received a letter from him in the previous week, she really poured on the guilt. These letters weren't specifically dated, but had to have been written in the mid 1880s. The other precious item was Grandma Clara's long, detailed description of their 1917 Idaho Christmas dinner, the one I recreated in 1977. Those documents became primary resources for my own family history project I wrote for the graduate class I was taking.

The day I was to return to Springfield, Mother fixed one of her delicious lunches. After that, I took a last tour of the house, visiting every room, looking in every closet. It was my way of saying goodbye to 40 memorable years there. In the end, it was finally easier to leave than I thought it would be.

There was amazingly little tension over who would get which items to be kept in the family. Marian was the recipient of two paintings -- one was an oil by Dad of Great

Aunt Jane that he had done from a photograph taken on her 100th birthday. The other was a large casein of Harper's Ferry by Hugo Pieper, a professional artist and friend that the folks had met the summer they went to visit the Saugatuck artist colony in Michigan. The only tension I recall was who would get Aunt Carrie's soup tureen, but even that was settled amicably.

A yard sale was held and two women, who organized such things, volunteered their services. That weekend event provided Dad with a great deal of amusement. Buyers wanted to meet the man who had owned the lawn mower. He asked Mother who bought the four-compartment ice cream freezer Uncle Walter Fredenhagen (owner of Prince Castle) had provided to us when frozen foods became the norm.

In the midst of this planned chaos were a number of farewell events, luncheons and coffee klatches. Harold White, Mother's editor at the *Sun*, hosted the final luncheon. As she was saying goodbye and thanking him for being so supportive all those 29 years, he said, "Genevieve, now you can freelance and still collect your pension. I'll take anything you write." He had not mentioned the possibility before, and this gift from heaven opened up wonderful possibilities. She could still keep writing.

Harold White announced this change in his *Dear Arch* column dated Aug. 4, 1977. He wrote, "There's good news this week and there's also bad news, Arch! First, the bad news. This is the last week that Genevieve Towsley's column, 'The Grapevine' will be published on a weekly basis. And sometime during August her monthly column, 'Sky-Lines' will appear for the last time on a regular schedule. And now the good news: Even though Genevieve and her hus-

Last Day at 417 S. Julian Street

band, Myron, will be leaving our community September 1, to live in a retirement home in Geneva (Batavia), she plans to write a 'Grapevine' column from time to time, perhaps once a month, and to do an occasional 'Sky-Lines' feature. We're sure her many followers will keep her informed on interesting tid-bits that will enable her to continue the writing for which she has gained much acclaim."

Mother scarcely missed a beat. She learned that it was not a long-distance call from Naperville to Batavia, which made her feel as if she'd just moved to a different Naperville location, not a different suburb. Her readers did as Harold had encouraged and continued to give her tidbits. Rarely a week went by that the *Sun* didn't carry one of her columns.

We three daughters, Betty from Malvern, Pa., Marian and I went to Batavia to help with the unpacking in mid-August, which was the weekend of Dad's 80th birthday. The five of us celebrated with a lovely dinner at the Mill Race Inn in Geneva. We four gray-haired women sang "Happy birthday, dear Daddy," because he was still Daddy to us. Later, a neighbor took our picture in front of the new fourplex home. That was the last time the five of us were together.

The folks managed to develop a workable routine. Mother planned to drop off her writing contribution at the *Sun* office on those 15-mile trips. Some weekdays she would drive back herself for an interview or to have lunch with friends. Because of Dad's increasing deafness and gradual memory losses, she started writing messages telling him where she would be or what was planned for their day in a 3-inch by 5-inch memo book, which I now have. On the first page, she put the names of their new friends

Marian, Betty, Caryl, Genevieve, Myron

At the Holmstad, Myron's 80th birthday

and neighbors, Ruby Keller and Katy Chapman and Ben Ryden. A little further in the book is: DIAL 4006 OR 4001 IF YOU WANT HELP.

On a typical page she wrote, "Gen goes to Nichols Library for interview then to Mary Lou Cowlishaw's for lunch." She left Mary Lou's phone number. If Mother had written the occasion and time for an upcoming event that both she and Dad were to attend, Dad wrote who would be there below it. She would plan to be home around 4 p.m. so they could share their "best time of the day," as she called it. Together, they would enjoy a glass of sherry and a few peanuts and catch up on the day's happenings as Dad smoked his pipe.

Eventually, Dad's health was such that Mother could no longer care for him at home. It was a difficult but mutual decision that he should be moved to Michaelson Health Center, the Holmstad's skilled nursing facility. The nurses and aides enjoyed having him there, and aside from an occasional period of confusion, he adjusted well. He always kept his sense of humor with a twinkle in his eye.

Mother used that little memo book even more after Dad moved to Michaelson because he seldom wore his hearing aid. In December 1984, Mother wanted to be in Springfield for our son, Eric's, wedding, which meant leaving Dad. The notebook page reads, "I am going to Eric's wedding Saturday, December 29 in Springfield. Will be home Sunday pm." The staff knew how long she would be gone, and she encouraged several friends to stop in to see him during that 36-hour period. When she got home, she found, "Myron you look handsome!" on the following page. She responded, "Who wrote this? Thanks. GT." The last note in the book reads, "On Tuesday July 9, Genevieve and the church secretary, Joy, will come to visit about 2 pm."

Dad enjoyed the occasional visits back to the fourplex on Sundays when Dick and I were able to be there. Pushing Dad in his wheelchair, Dick was able to get him across the Holmstad campus where Mother would serve one of her special meals like the one of beerbraten and noodles with buttered crumbs, ginger gravy and fresh asparagus. She prepared this meal for his 90th birthday on Aug. 18, 1985.

I visited Dad in Batavia in mid-October 1985. He told me he was thinking of taking piano lessons. I wheeled him into the Michaelson dining room where he plunked on a few piano keys before he told me he was ready to return to his room. Evidently he had a moderate stroke that night and died the following Friday, Oct. 25. By prearrangement, Dad was cremated. There was a lovely celebration of his life at First Congregational Church. His ashes were placed in a small grave in the northwest part of Naperville Cemetery.

After his death, Mother continued writing, which helped her handle the grief. The first holiday we celebrated was Thanksgiving at our home. Mother drove to Naperville to connect with Dick's sister, Joan Moy Smith, and the two of them drove to Springfield for our holiday dinner. Part of the day was spent listening to an old tape Dick had made with Dad in 1971 in which he told about his World War I experiences. Tearfully, Mother said, "I thought I'd never hear his voice again."

The two drove back to Naperville the next day, getting there in the late afternoon. A cold front was predicted, and the weather was worsening, but Mother was ready to get home. She had writing to do!

Dick and I had been out that Friday evening, and we came home to an alarming message on the answer machine, "Geneveieve Towsley has been in an auto accident. Please call Delnor Hospital in St. Charles." As my heart sank, I did as directed and later called her minister, Keith Torney. The only information the hospital would tell us was that she was in intensive care with a concussion and multiple broken bones from a one-car accident. The Rev. Torney braved icy roads and drove to Delnor in St. Charles that evening. Because of the weather, we were not able to get there until the next day. Even in her semiconscious state, her usual pluck and determination came through. "You can't keep Genevieve down!" she said emphatically. In addition to the concussion, she had three fractures in her pelvis and seven cracked ribs. The accident had occurred on her favorite route home, Batavia Road, through the grounds of Fermi Laboratories where she hit an icy spot. The car had wrapped around a tree and the Fermilab Fire Department rescued her by cutting her out of the vehicle.

Both Marian and I, with the help of our Naperville cousin, Rita Harvard, were able to handle the many necessary details of her recovery, including getting her new glasses. She wanted a "visitor notebook," in which friends could tell her they had been there if she was asleep, or having tests, or simply not remembering the visit. She had no memory of the accident. Her recovery was slow, but we were able to celebrate Christmas with her back at Michaelson.

In early January, she returned to Delnor with cardiac arrhythmia. By this time, she had been writing again. I knew her old spunk had kicked in when I read the Jan. 15, 1986, *Grapevine* column where she promoted a Women's

Health Conference at Delnor. It was not only a message to her readers that she was going to attend that conference on Feb. 8, but I think it was also a message to me to be prepared.

She wrote, "All winter long I had Feb. 8 marked on my calendar, for that is the date of the Women's Self Health Conference, sponsored by Delnor Community Health Care Foundation. Our daughter, Caryl Moy, has been scheduled as one of the seminar speakers. She will speak on "Getting in Touch with Sensuality and Sexual Values." Caryl is on the faculties of Sangamon State University and Southern Illinois University and has a private practice as a family and sex therapist. Although she has given presentations before professional societies throughout the country, I have never heard her, and want to avail myself of the opportunity on Feb. 8. To achieve that goal I'll have to become stronger, but my niece, Rita Harvard, will help with transportation."

She closed by telling her readers that the conference was open to all women and what number to call for information. Within a week, she was back in Michaelson.

I realized having her at the conference was going to be a little awkward for me. I would be talking about sexuality with my 79-year-old mother in the audience. I would have the discomfort of being in the dual roles of professor and daughter. At least if Rita could get her there, I could concentrate on being professional. Unfortunately, Rita had a conflict and wouldn't be able to bring her. Now I truly had a dual role of lecturer and caregiver.

In what was not my softest directive style, I told Mother I would take her, but she had to be at the Michaelson entrance, dressed and ready to go with her walker by 8:30.

She was! We headed north to the conference setting, but I was very quiet, feeling both irritated and anxious. Tenderly, she laid her hand on my knee and said, "I love you, Caryl. I've looked forward to this day for a long time." I patted her knee in return and thought, "Whatever happens, it'll be all right." My anxiety and resentment had been replaced by love and self-confidence and a bit of guilt.

I began by introducing Mother and telling the audience how this was her first "outing" since her life threatening accident. It was a most significant event for her and for me. Just saying this lowered some of my anxiety. She was given a large applause. I began as I often did by asking the group to think about their own attitudes and beliefs about sexuality. To facilitate this, I asked for six to eight women, who would be willing to take a position along an invisible continuum of an agree-disagree scale as I would read statements representing the common ranges of opinions on various aspects of sexual behavior. Eight women volunteered. Some of the statements included, "I have to have a love relationship in order to have a sexual relationship," "I would want my 14-year-old child to have access to birth control," "I think homosexuals should be allowed to marry." I encouraged the audience to make a mental note of where they would stand on each of the value statements. The audience was quick to respond to the experience with laughter and questions. Discussion easily followed on the difference between sensuality and sexuality and how sex is only a part of sexuality.

Mother said very little. Her reaction seemed to be, "What's the big deal?" Talking about sex never had been a problem for her. Afterwards, I received a lot of positive comments from participants I saw at lunch or in the halls.

In looking back on the occasion, I realized that particular presentation was one of my best.

She continued to recover from the accident and was back in her fourplex within a month. We arranged to bring her a replacement car from Springfield. Behind the wheel again, she was a little nervous for about 10 minutes, but soon was handling the road comfortably. Later that spring, she flew to California to visit her nephew, Brayton, and several friends. In August, she drove herself to Springfield to attend an Elder Hostel program and visit us for several days.

Her life seemed to be getting back to what it had been before the accident, but then late on a Saturday afternoon, she took a tumble outside the fourplex and was unable to get up without help. It was nearly an hour before someone found her. I urged her to move to an apartment in the complex so more people would be around to help. She finally agreed, but this move was difficult for her. She went from a two-bedroom apartment to one. The bedroom suite she owned since she was married had to go. The kitchen for her use was small because residents could choose to eat one meal a day in the main dining room. She gave away her many cookbooks.

On my first day of summer break in mid-June 1988, I received an early morning phone call from her former neighbor, Katherine Chapman. They always called each other morning and night to signal that they were okay. Mother had been taken to Delnor again because she had fallen the night before and her hip had fractured. She lay there several hours before she could move herself enough to reach the phone to call for help.

And so we began another recovery period, first in Delnor, then again in Michaelson. Yet, she still managed to keep writing. She had her telephone, and Naperville friends brought her news. Irene Tindall, features editor at the *Sun*, accepted what she wrote in long hand. Rita Harvard, who all along has seemed more like a daughter than a niece, was there at least weekly, took care of her laundry, and delivered her columns to the *Sun*. I was only able to visit every week or two, so I very much appreciated all the support that Rita, the Michaelson staff and the Congregational Church provided.

By early fall, it became obvious that she was not going to be able to manage living alone in her apartment. She now needed a walker all of the time. She was quite happy to be moved to Colonial House, the assisted living facility, at the Holmstad. This meant further downsizing to one room, but she could take all her own remaining furnishings. She still had her telephone, her favorite pens from Beidelman-Kunsch Funeral Home and notebooks. She gave her car to Marian because she could no longer drive. Rita assisted in this move, making it all go smoothly, because I was in China representing Southern Illinois University School of Medicine at its sister medical school at Sun Yat Sen University in Guangzho, China. Because Dick is so violently allergic to peanuts he doesn't dare travel in Asia.

Feeling a bit guilty for not being there for the move, I was able to call one evening. Because there was a 12-hour time difference, I hoped I could catch her before she went to breakfast. In this time before cell phones, we had an amazingly good connection. I apparently couldn't have given her a better present! She proudly announced at breakfast that she had gotten a call from China that morning.

We had purchased a folding walker, which made it possible for her to still go out with friends. Many brought her to Naperville for special occasions. Some people came to see her or to be interviewed. Through the years, there were increasing physical limitations. We could tell she had had a mini-stroke or two because her facial contours had changed a bit.

A Colonial House requirement was that the resident must be able to walk with a walker to the dining room. When she could barely do that in the fall of 1993, the Holmstad staff told me she would have to be moved to Michaelson permanently. The move needed to be made the following weekend. I had to be the one to tell her.

Her first reaction was, "What more do I have to live for?" Holding back tears myself, I tried to give her a loving response, "You still have Rita and John, and you have us and the grandchildren, and all your Naperville friends." She knew she had no choice and resigned herself to the move and loss of her last furnishings.

Marian came from St. Louis to get some tables. Our son, Philip, who was living in nearby Warrenville, came with his pick-up truck and took the furniture items that he and his brother, Eric, wanted. The Holmstad took the ones the family didn't want. She could take one dresser and clothes that would fit into a small closet. All her jewelry was the costume variety. Choosing what to keep was the hardest task for her. I kept a few of the remaining items that I had given her and she hadn't selected. Today, whenever I put on the pewter sheep pin or the grapevine brooch, I still remember that sad day.

I was pitching empty boxes when one of them rattled as I tossed it. In it were two tiny porcelain ducks I hadn't seen in over 20 years. They were the first items that I was assigned to dust as a child. They are now part of my large miniature village display. Since then, I have become an avid collector of miniature porcelain buildings, and every visiting viewer hears that story.

We arranged to have her own phone installed and bought her an answering machine. She was back in business within the week. Even though Mother's health worsened, she was determined to keep writing. She said, "When I'm writing, the pain and worry go away." She knew many readers waited each week to read what she wrote and she wanted to provide similar articles that they had loved to see for the past 40 years. That, along with the love and support of the *Sun* staff, kept her going long after others would have given up.

If she didn't have Naperville news, she wrote about interesting people she met at Michaelson. There was an elderly couple, each over 100. Every evening, the husband watched "Wheel of Fortune" hoping to guess the answer before the contestants did. There were two single ladies, who at each meal loudly talked about how glad they were to be there and have each other. It was painful to watch her struggle to walk to the dining room with her walker. She would give herself half an hour to get there. Finally, she grudgingly used a wheelchair, but that took a different kind of strength than she was used to using, so it, too, was slow going.

In June 1994, on one of my visits, I took a large box of old photos for her to sort through and identify the location and who the people in them were. The Michaelson staff gave us a vacant office that day. I was so delighted when she went through them as though she had taken the photo yesterday. After sorting through the photographs, we went to the new Holmstad restaurant, and I wheeled her to the beauty shop. For me, it was a memorable day.

Six weeks later, when I told her we were all going to that restaurant to celebrate our 40th wedding anniversary, she didn't remember the occasion. On the actual anniversary, August 21st, the Michaelson staff had her dressed appropriately, and we were able to get her to the first Congregational Church where Dick and I had been married. That was the last time she attended a service there.

Gradually, she produced fewer columns, and these were less unique than her former ones. The *Sun* graciously accepted what she wrote, but in June 1994, her *Grapevine* column appeared for the last time. It concluded with her familiar words "Till next time," followed by her signature, Genevieve Towsley. Even then her intentions were to continue writing.

She faded slowly. On her 88th birthday, Feb. 3, 1995, a dozen caring friends from Naperville's First Congregational Church brought coffeecakes for a birthday celebration. She was so weak I had to feed her, but her eyes were still sparkling. She died quietly on March 6, 1995.

19

Honors and Recognitions

I have talked about the honors Genevieve received while attending North Central (North Western) College, including second place in a regional speech contest and graduating with high honors. But from 1928 until she began writing in 1948, the only opportunity she had to display her talents as a wordsmith was writing the centennial history in 1933 of the First Congregational Church. Through the years, she still referred to that history. She received her first honor for journalism in 1952 when writing for the *Naperville Clarion.* Her article about Professor Guy Oliver I told about in "the Clarion Years" was recognized by the Illinois Press Association as best feature story the previous year.

There was growing respect for her unique writing style from readers as she took on controversial topics that she said were "for the public good." She highlighted issues of poverty, medical care for migrant workers and homelessness. But other than compliments she received personally, there was no public recognition of this until the book of her columns, *A View of Historic Naperville*, was published in 1975. This volume became a community treasure and many came to realize that Genevieve Towsley's talent was a gift to the city. In February 1976, American Legion, Post Number 43 presented her with the Citizen of the Year Award. The elaborate certificate reads, "Genevieve Towsley is awarded this Certificate in Recognition of an Outstanding Service To His Fellow Man." Obviously when the Legion had certificates printed, it was assumed any person deserving that award would have to be a man.

One month later in March 1976, the Naperville Branch of the American Association of University Women on the occasion of their 20th anniversary honored her at a tea for her "community service in the field of journalism."

The next year, in February 1977, Chairman of the Board of Illinois Benedictine University, the Rev. Daniel W. Kucera, sent the most glowing letter to congratulate her on her article about Father Francis, one of the university's founders, who was a significant leader in the most stressful of times. He called the article "a masterpiece" and went on to say, "God has given you a great talent and you use it for the pleasure of so many of us effectively."

In fall of 1977, the story about her pioneer childhood in Idaho story received an award from the Northern Illinois Press Association for best feature of 1976 by an Illinois writer.

Of all the special recognitions she received, she was most proud of the honorary degree, Doctor of Letters, awarded by North Central College at its June 1978 commencement, which was held outside in front of Old Main. The weather was pleasantly warm with sunshine, all of which added to the celebration.

The doctorate was "in recognition of her contributions as a journalist, historian of community and church, leader in human relations, wife and mother," read Dr. Richard Eastman, who was the professor and chair of general studies. "Anyone living in Naperville during the last generation has heard the voice of Genevieve Towsley in the *Naperville Sun*. There, she has celebrated through her columns and articles the diverse talents, achievements and traditions of our townspeople.

"Thus, she has made hundreds of us visible to each other. Everyone here should take pride in remembering that Genevieve graduated from this college in 1928. She is a model for this whole surrounding area to see the kind of women and men our alma mater can send out."

In her acceptance speech, she made special mention of the two men in her life. Without them, she knew she would never have been in a position to receive such an honor. One of course was Dad. "Myron has always been with me with support and encouragement in my community concerns and my writings," she said, "There is my editor, Harold White. Harold gave me a special kind of freedom to write whatever and however I saw fit."

She finished on a nostalgic note. "Today is a very special anniversary for me, for 50 years ago this weekend, June 12, 1928, I marched across Pfeiffer Hall stage and received my bachelor's degree. So this event becomes a truly golden anniversary."

Of course we called her Doctor Towsley for a few days. Each time she heard that she had the typical reflex answer,

"Doctor Towsley"

"Who's that?" But then she would smile with pride. By the end of the week she was just "Genevieve" again.

The following year, North Central named her the Outstanding Alum for 1979. She prepared an acceptance speech for that event. Then, less than five days before the event, she tripped on a piece of outdoor carpeting on the fourplex patio and fell on her face. Several teeth were knocked out. Her face was badly bruised, and the doctor ordered her confined to care at Colonial House. She asked niece, Rita Harvard, to give the speech in her place, which, of course, Rita did, but not before Mother had her rehearse it in front of her three times.

In December 1985, the Naperville Community Chorus honored her at their winter concert by making her an honorary member of the chorus for all the written support she had provided for that group. Several years earlier she had put one item in *The Grapevine* column announcing the formation of the chorus and how those interested might join. Regularly, there were announcements about concerts in the years that followed. Unfortunately, she couldn't attend that 1985 honoring performance because she was in intensive care following her near fatal car accident.

She even received accolades for that event, receiving the "Saved By The Belt" award from the State of Illinois. The Illinois seat belt law had gone into effect in July 1985. To promote seat belt use, then Secretary of State Jim Edgar, sponsored a contest for the best stories of how a seat belt saved a life. Members of the rescue squad that cut her out of the car that fateful November evening were sure she would have been killed if she hadn't been wearing her seat belt. Three of those awards were given in the spring of 1986 and Mother was one of the recipients. The Harvards,

Rita and her husband John, took her into Chicago to McCormick Place, and with a wheelchair, pushed her to the awards luncheon. She received a handsome wristwatch, a "Saved by the Belt" pin, and an impressive certificate.

On August 3, 1986, Nichols Library in downtown Naperville sponsored a Genevieve Towsley Appreciation Day in her honor to acknowledge "her years of contribution to the community." There was a reception, and several people spoke, giving very complimentary remarks. Her publisher, Harold White, gave a presentation. A proclamation from the mayor was read. Guests were encouraged to bring their personal copies of *A View of Historic View Naperville*. The invitation read, "Mrs. Towsley has graciously agreed to autograph copies of her book."

I was sorry that the library chose the one Sunday of the year that I had to be out of the country. Our family had made the reservation a year ahead to be in Canada that week, but Rita again stepped in, taking her to purchase a new dress, and with John, drove her to the library. She was given a corsage, and photos showed she looked radiant.

It was in 1989 when the DuPage County Sesquicentennial Steering Committee named Mother as one of 150 citizens who played a major role in the county's 150 year history. When asked about this she thought it was overstating things. She said, "I'm not one who shapes worlds. I've just tried to be a catalyst, to present good things when they came along."

In 1993, the Illinois Department of Aging honored 73 women in Illinois, 85 years or older, who were still making contributions to their community. Mara Lee Lindley, director of the department, said, "A desire to help others doesn't necessarily diminish late in life." Each woman received a certificate of Lifetime Achievement, signed by Lindley and Illinois First Lady, Brenda Edgar, hailing them as role models and calling their contributions "History in the Making." Kathy Millen from the *Sun* wrote the feature about the four Naperville women who were among the 73 honorees.

Of course, at her memorial service, there were many tributes to her, which warmed our hearts and helped ease the pain of her loss. But her loss affected not only our family, but the larger family of readers and community members who enjoyed her work and, through her words, perhaps were encouraged to make a difference in their hometown. Her spirit continues to live on through her writing and in our hearts.

20
Others' Thoughts

During the process of writing these memoirs, several of Genevieve's friends and admirers commented that she was such a special person to them. Glenna Holloway, Tim West and Rita Harvard gave their thoughts to Donna DeFalco for inclusion in this chapter.

Glenna Holloway is the friend and colleague who kept Mother supplied with spiral bound stenographer pads when she was no longer able to drive to get her own supply of paper. One of those pads is bronzed with the Century Walk sculpture. Glenna describes Genevieve as a consummate journalist with contacts throughout the community who would keep her up-to-date on all the news. It's no surprise that when Glenna Holloway moved to Naperville in 1973, Mother would find out that an award-winning poet had come to town. Glenna has had her work published in *McCall's, Ladies Home Journal, Saturday Evening Post, Notre Dame Review,* and many other publications.

The native of Nashville, Tenn., moved to Naperville when her husband was transferred to this area. They purchased a home in the Farmstead subdivision because, as Glenna said, "This was country and we loved that."

Glenna tells, "After Genevieve's cheery greeting, 'Welcome to Naperville,' we two writers talked on the telephone, and I was impressed with Genevieve's charming and thorough interviewing style. She featured me as a newcomer to Naperville in *The Grapevine* column.

After our initial conversation, we became friends and enjoyed many conversations together. I liked to get her started because she was a fountain of information. She remembered everything. She had a marvelous memory."

Seventeen years after their first interview, Glenna returned the favor when she was a freelance writer for the *Chicago Tribune*. On December 2, 1990, in The Tempo DuPage section of the Sunday Tribune was Glenna's article, "You Probably Heard It On '*The Grapevine*'. It featured Mother's more than 40 years of chronicling Naperville.

Glenna called her "the *grande dame* of writing."

In 2006, Glenna was commissioned by the Young Naperville Singers to write the lyrics for the song that celebrated the 175th Anniversary of Naperville's founding. She used Genevieve's book, *A View of Historic Naperville*, as a reference for her work.

"She had an interest in people and history," Glenna said. "She was a remarkable person and I think everyone who ever met her liked her."

One of Mother's *Naperville Sun* colleagues, Tim West, was 26 years old when he started at the newspaper in 1973. He was a graduate student at the University of Cincinnati and worked as a part-time photographer in the summer.

Editor Harold White offered the graduate student in Western Civilization a full-time job at the end of the summer. Tim had always loved the newspaper business having worked on high school and college newspapers, so he accepted the offer. He recalled that at the time, the newsroom was mostly married women, who worked part-time.

"We knew everybody, and we sat together in this big bullpen," he said. "There were no offices. Even Harold didn't have an office."

Tim says, "As a young reporter I thought Genevieve was good at writing stories that were favorable to the community, but I also knew that she wasn't afraid to tackle important social issues of the day, such as integration."

"She wasn't afraid to ruffle some feathers if she thought somebody was being wronged," he says. Today Tim is commentary editor at the *Sun,* and he continues to rely on Genevieve's book, *A View of Historic Naperville,* when he needs to look up historic information.

"If I want to know something about Naperville's history, I hope she has it in her book," he says. "It's a standard reference."

Tim credits, as I do, longtime *Sun* staffer Peg Sproul with putting the book together, including editing and choosing the photographs.

"If it weren't for Genevieve, there wouldn't be an historic book," Tim said. "She dug up all that information, examined all those documents and talked to all those old-timers before they passed on. She did all those stories on historic Naperville that no one else was doing." Also, if it weren't for Peg Sproul there wouldn't be an historic book, for it was she who put the stories and photos together in publishable form."

Dr. Michael Ebner is the one who can speak with the greatest authority about how unique it is for a community to have a "voice" such as Genevieve's. I've mentioned Dr. Ebner before. He is the retired history professor from Lake Forest College who has studied "edge communities" focusing on the comparison of Naperville to Princeton, New Jersey and Palo Alto, California. He read her columns in *The Sun* through the years and says, "Naperville enjoyed hearing her voice and it was a respected voice. Her chronicling influenced the community to think globally."

Mary Lou Cowlishaw and Genevieve were colleagues at *The Sun* in the late 1970s. They seldom were in the office at the same time, but when their paths would cross there, each would pause where the other one was working, talk about their latest project, who they had just interviewed or they would just catch up on each other's lives. Cowlishaw remembers that she enjoyed hearing Genevieve laugh. "It was so spontaneous and infectious," she says.

Mary Lou Cowlishaw is the outstanding 41st District representative to the Illinois legislature from Naperville who served from 1982-2002, always an advocate for education. She and Genevieve are two of the women featured in the Channel 17 documentary, "A Role of Her Own." Presently, she is an adjunct professor of education at North Central College. She is the first person I heard describe Mother as a "wordsmith," one who uses words skillfully.

In our conversation, I mentioned that I can find no one who has ever written a negative word about Mother. Mary Lou, responded, "I'm not surprised. Nobody has anything unkind to say about Genevieve. She was such a warm, caring person, one with whom others felt very comfortable, even those who are different."

All of the comments from those I've talked with who were involved with the formation of The Naperville Heritage Society almost put her in the "saint" category. Helen Fraser, was a volunteer at Martin Mitchell Museum. She came to Naperville when her husband's work brought them to the area. To get better acquainted in the community, she volunteered at the museum. Her background was in history and preservation so she soon became a valued employee as the curator of Martin Mitchell Museum. Referring to Mother, she said, "She was so helpful to me in my research. She always found time to talk to me. Once your mother moved to The Holmstad, she frequently invited me to come over to talk about what I needed to know. Of course, then she served those delicious cinnamon pecan rolls. Helen wrote the walking guide, "Footsteps through Old Naperville" and dedicated it to Genevieve. After I talked with Mrs. Fraser, she thoughtfully sent me the thank you note she had saved that Mother wrote to her at least 20 years ago, when she learned of the dedication. Genevieve's final words to her were, "Thank you, dear friend, for all you mean to me and to Naperville." It's obvious they both valued each other's friendship.

Peg Yonker wrote the charming story, "Lone Feather and The Settlers, A History of Naperville." In her acknowledgements in this book she credits Mother as being the discoverer of Hannah Ditzler's diaries which were the inspiration for her book. (I didn't realize that Mother was the one who found those, probably in the Martin-Mitchell maid's room archive) In the Heritage Society's early years Peg became the director, volunteering nearly full time

Peg Yonker, Genevieve Towsley, Helen Fraser

At Martin-Mitchell Museum

until the organization was fiscally able to hire a full-time professional director, Peggy Frank. Peg spoke of the many times she called Mother for her wisdom and advice in this interim.

Peggy Frank, Executive Director of Naper Settlement, Naperville Heritage Society has said , "Your mother made lasting contributions not only in recording the oral history of our community but chronicling much about the change of our town. I felt privileged to have known her and called her a friend."

Family friend, Willard Smith, is a retired professor of studio arts and jewelry at College of DuPage. He held that position for 25 years and credits Genevieve with telling him of the faculty position at COD. He had been teaching in the public schools in the Denver area in the 1960s but was hoping to get a position back in the Naperville area. It was at a family holiday dinner that Mother told him about the vacancy. He has always been grateful that she was the catalyst in his getting the job.

Barbara Nelson is Mother's niece, her brother Merle's daughter, and she and her husband, Bob, live in Crystal Lake, Illinois. Barbara says, "I remember what gracious hosts Aunt Genevieve and Uncle Myron were when we went to their home for a meal or a visit. They consistently made you feel so special and were always glad you could come.

When Uncle Myron was in the nursing home, she would take over their sherry in a pint jar and have it out in the hall away from others. She wished there would be a room just for seniors who still liked to cuddle, kiss and hug. So she talked to the "powers that be" at the Holmstad and the cuddle room was born. Only my Aunt Gen would do that! When we were helping her on one of her moves, she gave me a small metal lamp that she would no longer be using. It hangs over our kitchen table. It's like having a little bit of Aunt Gen with us each morning. She was a grand lady!"

Rita Harvard is another loving niece. I've mentioned her many times before in this story. Her mother, Grace, was my Dad's sister. Her father, Walter Fredenhagen, owned the ice cream company where my Dad was advertising manager. They are the couple who in 1939, completely restored the historic Bailey Hobson house. The Hobson house was in the country so Rita especially enjoyed visiting us, her Aunt Genevieve, Uncle Myron, and my sister Marian and me in what she called downtown Naperville, 417 South Julian Street.

She remembers, "The aroma that hit you when you came in the front door was just heaven," Rita said. "I always felt very comfortable and safe there."

Rita said she always felt like another daughter to Genevieve.

"She was really my surrogate mother," she said. "I was 34 when my mother died. I really wished Caryl was my sister." (The feeling was mutual.)

When we were in high school, Rita and I both volunteered as guides at the Martin-Mitchell Museum where we enjoyed taking visitors on tours of the Victorian mansion.

Rita says, "As Aunt Genevieve started writing her newspaper column, I began reading the articles and loved them. The article that made the biggest impression on me was one that described an asphalt plant, which was planned to be built next to the Kroehler Manufacturing Company.

"I remember going door-to-door in the Kroehler subdivision and telling the people they had to rise up against it. The public outcry didn't fall on deaf ears, and the City Council quickly voted down the proposed asphalt plant.

In so many ways, Aunt Genevieve was ahead of her time," Rita said.

Our families remained close throughout the years and when Mother and Dad moved to the Holmstad in Batavia, Rita helped whenever she was needed. She made their care so pleasant. I am particularly grateful for all she did when Mother was in Colonial House shelter care and Michaelson Health Center, the nursing home. She did her laundry, brought her personal necessities, and delivered her hand-written columns to *The Sun* each week. making it possible for her to keep writing.

"She was so used to getting that weekly paycheck," Rita said. "She would give me the article in an envelope, and I would put it in the drop box at the *Sun*."

Rita thinks that the bronze statue seated on the corner of Chicago and Washington in downtown Naperville captures the soul of her Aunt Genevieve. With notebook in hand, pen raised ready to write, Naperville's Genevieve is still on the job, providing inspiration to the hundreds of visitors and residents who pass by every day.

Rita says, "Everyone should have an Aunt Genevieve."

I say, "Everyone should have a cousin Rita."

❈ 21 ❈
Her Spirit Lives On

As Mother had requested, Reverend Keith Torney returned to Naperville from Montana to bury her ashes next to Dad's, and to preach the memorial service meditation in her beloved First Congregational Church. Marian and I both agreed that the hymn, In the Garden, should be one of the musical selections. (It had been part of the music at both Grandma Clara's funeral and at Dad's.) Torney used the Garden theme in his meditation. Referring to her historical writing, he said, "She told us of gardens of our past, reminding us how great our agricultural heritage was. She told us of other gardens, ones that could have been walled off." (These referred to her articles introducing us to new people from other cultures.) "She showed us what our gardens could be." He commented on her sense of honesty. "Industrial Gypsies" she used for the new church members whose companies transferred them away when they had been in Naperville barely a year. Keith told that he was asked to request that she refrain from using that term. He explained that, "In wisdom beyond my years I told them I would not."

Three other pastors also participated; Robert Baggat, senior pastor, Sally Owen Still, associate pastor of First Congregational, and David Foxriver, pastor of the Batavia Congregational Church, where Mother had been an associate member. Our son, Philip, commented afterwards how unique the service was, that he'd never been to a funeral where there were four preachers or where someone spoke how she had "legitimatized" his marriage.

As was the custom in that church, the congregation was invited to share their memories of Genevieve. The first to take the microphone was a woman who remembered the Sunday that the sermon had been about the woman who had been caught in adultery and the "talk back" session that followed. Mother was the first to respond, asking the question, "What happened to the man?" Smiling, I thought, "Social justice was always on Mother's mind."

North Central College president, Harold Wilde began his very touching remarks with "Genevieve Brayton, class of 1928—Genevieve Brayton Towsley, Class of Naperville. She intertwined North Central and the community through her writing. She embodied the best of what this community means."

Later, of course, while all of the special comments and the notes of sympathy were appreciated, it was hard to finally realize that I was an orphan. I wanted to call her on the phone and tell her of a memory some one had shared or of our latest family events. Our dear cousin, Rita Harvard, was executor of her "estate," and handled the legal parts of that with love and competence.

Memories continued to interrupt several times a day as I grieved our loss. One helpful distraction was my new hobby of collecting Christmas Village buildings, the ones of porcelain that make an impressive scene when lit. For Christmas 1996, Department 56, the village company, issued the accessory set, "Bringing Fleeces to the Mill." It featured a little girl leading a sheep. When Dick saw that piece, he said, "That's Genevieve!" His comment was the inspiration for the centerpiece village display I created to represent her most memorable Christmas, the one she described so vividly in her Idaho childhood story. I obtained enough figures to represent her and her mother delivering homemade presents to the neighbors. I fashioned her red hooded bathrobe out of a piece of red flannel. I photo-copied early photos of her and pasted them on to the milk wagon to create the school wagon. My grandson Ben, then age nine, strung tiny pieces of Styrofoam popcorn to decorate the sagebrush branches. Then he put the little glass ornaments on it and we had our Idaho Christmas tree. Off to one side I put Uncle "Merle," later known as "Bill," with his trunk beside him, leaving the farm, that he had "proved up." And of course there were lots of miniature sheep. I bought several extra sets of those. As it turned out, it was a wonderful way to grieve. When I would describe the scene to visitors, I usually had a tear or two. Dick encouraged me to enter it in a display contest at the annual Department 56 Gathering the following summer. With added background of original Idaho photos, appropriate trees and other animals, I packed it up, drove with a friend to Minneapolis the following August and set it up once more in my assigned booth. I placed a photo portrait of Genevieve along with copies of her story beside it. It won third place for large displays. I was thrilled. When back in Springfield we reset the display in our "village room." I could finally talk about her and her Idaho story and not tear up. I could also brag about her.

In 1995, the year of her death our country was beginning to prepare for the Millennium and worrying if our modern digital accounting systems would handle Y2K. In Naperville, ever conscious of its past, a Century Walk Corporation was formed to pay tribute to Naperville's significant local people, places and events of the 20th century. The plan was to commission various artists and sculptors over a ten-year period to create large outdoor art pieces, representing this concept. The goal was to have 30 pieces, three a year, painted on building walls and sculptures along the River Walk or along the streets of Naperville. It was to be funded with a hotel guest tax, private contributions and a grant from the Illinois Arts Council. The 13 member group, chaired by attorney Brand Bobosky, decided to include one life-size sculpture of a Naperville citizen whose life and work best represented the 20th century of Naperville. Genevieve had written over 150 historic articles about the city from 1948-1994, so it is easy to see why she was the corporation's choice. The corporation asked Rita to call to tell us Mother was selected. I was so elated, I slept very little that night.

The sculptor selected for the job was Pamela S. Carpenter of Sculpit Studio. She was the perfect choice for the job. A statement about her work reads, "Pamela goes beyond the obvious, not wishing to imitate what her eye sees, but what her heart, mind and soul feel in a single magnified moment." Pamela had previously lived in Naperville, so she knew about Mother but had never met her.

She was honored that she was the selected sculptor. Rita encouraged her to, "Meet and talk with Caryl. She looks so much like Genevieve."

Pamela's phone call to me started a rewarding experience. She asked me to send any photos or videos of her, circa 1980. She planned to create her as she looked about that time. She planned to have her seated and taking notes. I sent her a box full of photographs and one video. These prompted many questions from her: Do you have the sweater with the grapevines you had embroidered on it? Do you have the glasses she wore then? When was she born? Do you have Genevieve's wedding ring or a picture of it? Do you have actual notes she wrote for the Grapevine?

To one question the answer was, "No, due to being badly stained, I didn't have the actual sweater, but I did have one of a similar texture she could use. Pamela took that and embroidered a grapevine on it, herself. I was able to send a similar pair of glasses to those she wore in 1980. The original pair had been destroyed in her car accident. She was born in 1907. My sister Marian now had her ring. I could send a picture of mine which was similar. She wanted to have actual notes in Mother's handwriting on the pad she would be holding. I found a partially used stenographer's pad where she had written, "Naperville has grown big and fat."

We arranged a date for us to get together at her Warrenville studio. When we walked in, "Genevieve" surrounded us. Pamela had enlarged the photos I had sent to poster size and attached them to her walls. That day she took over 100 photos of me and parts of my arms and legs and almost an equal number of measurements, like thumb length, measurement from knee to ankle, or elbow to shoulder. She told me, "Much work goes into this sculpture even before I begin building the armature." She surrounded herself with images, so that when she would begin sculpting she could, "almost do it with her eyes closed." In November of 1998, six months before the unveiling date, Pamela invited those members of the Century Walk Corporation who had known Mother well, Dee Pasternak, Willard Smith and Pat Springer as well as Rita and John, to come to her studio to make any suggestions to make the statue more like Genevieve. Their reaction was so positive; the only change suggested was the crook of one finger.

In his next Christmas note, Willard (Bill) Smith wrote that it was so exciting to be on the Century Walk board and watch Genevieve's statue come to life. He knew Pamela had done a lot of research. He described the process so well. "I suppose you know, when she finishes the clay work she'll make two plaster casts; turn one over to the foundry. They'll make a wax model which she will cut into about 18 pieces with a hot wire. Each of those will be cast in bronze separately and she will weld them together, grind, sand and polish every seam! Whew! We're getting a bargain!" (Bill is a former professor of studio arts and jewelry at College of DuPage.) He volunteered to be a committee of one for art maintenance for the Century Walk projects.

The first section finished was the legs which "blew up" in the process. There was time to redo them but great concern if other sections did the same. None did.

Early in June, 1999, a large plastic wrapped bundle was wrestled out of the back of Joe Powers' pickup truck and carried across the sidewalk to an empty stone bench next to the front door of Barnes and Noble. Powers and

Rick Gurrieri attracted a few stares. Didn't that look like a body? A crowd gathered to watch. One mother turned to her young daughter and said, "There's going to be a statue there--see her feet?" The sandaled toes had become unwrapped. Pamela was there to be sure no more came unwrapped and to supervise the attachment to the bench. Once it was certain that the wrapped Genevieve was securely attached, she was left until the unveiling on June 19th. In that brief interim, one person reported to the police a homeless person all wrapped in plastic was sitting in front of Barnes and Noble.

Even though it was a rainy day, June 13th was a glorious day. Until Pamela pulled the purple ribbon, the audience remained in the book store. There were brief remarks by Brand Bobosky and former legislator, Mary Lou Cowlishaw, among others. I told the group I had this great urge to call Mother to tell her about the occasion so she could write about it. (That old feeling has never left.)

Before she pulled the ribbon, Pamela read a poem that she had written to go with the sculpture.

"Genevieve."
Come sit with Genevieve
If you may,
She'll lend her ear
to what you say.
She "pounded the pavement"
And upon her search
This journalist wrote of
community, county and church.
Her stories meandered through

our everyday life
Writing of our neighbors'
Joys and strife.
Like the fruited vine
Upon arbor sound
Her columns became our
History in written bound
Come sit with Genevieve
If you may
She's a 20th century icon
In every way

Pamela S. Carpenter, Poet and Sculpist

A bronze plaque with these words would be attached later to the brick wall behind the statue.

My first reaction on seeing the statue was, "How inviting it is!" It beckons one to sit beside her to look at what she is writing. Her arthritic bronze hand holds her favorite pen, one of the many supplied to her by Beidelman-Kunsch Funeral Services. She has written again, "Naperville has grown big and fat," in the spiral bound notebook in her lap. She is wearing a light weight cardigan sweater embroidered with a grapevine on each side of the front opening.

Generally the reactions to this new town feature were positive. A few letters to editors thought she needed to be in a more dignified place and on a pedestal. Others countered that the placement was perfect that she would want to be where the action was. We were shocked when we learned that her glasses had been pulled off by vandals soon after she was put in place. The committee and Pamela agreed that it was probably best to leave them off and that the

Pamela Carpenter, Sculpist, with the Genevieve statue and Caryl Towsley Moy

small drainage holes where they attached could function better without being covered.

She was soon a familiar meeting point. Teenagers riding bikes from different directions would say, "I'll meet you at Granny." When winter came, North Central students put a NCC stocking cap and scarf on her. One Naperville North High School student wrote that he couldn't get a date for the prom so he asked her. Whenever we could get to Naperville, it was always heartwarming to see a couple of bicycles leaning against her bench or a mother with a baby in her lap sitting beside her. Her old friend, Beverly Patterson Frier, told me she always says "hi!" to her when she walks by. Adam and Debbie Cohen wrote while they never knew Genevieve, they have read her book many times and their children enjoy climbing to sit beside her to read what the statue is writing.

One day when I was standing by the statue, a grandmother who was visiting in Naperville tried to explain to her grandchildren who she was. Of course, I quickly gave her the answer. Another time, one man, who didn't know the story, joked, "She's been waiting for a bus for a long time." There were other similar comments of puzzlement. Rita and I soon realized that nowhere was her full name given and that if one hadn't known how significant she was, the reason for her being there would soon be lost.

Then in January 2000 the Chicago SunTimes had an article on Chicago area community art projects. A photo of Brand Bobosky was shown by the statue telling the reporter the statue was of Genevieve Towsley, a Naperville journalist, author and historian. I thought that was the perfect identifier. Rita and I decided to ask The Centennial Walk Corporation to install a new plaque. I asked

Brand what would have happened to that story if he hadn't been there to talk to the reporter. We made some wording suggestions including Brand's quote. We also suggested that "1907-1995," the years she lived be added after her full name. At first the group didn't want to make any changes, but when I pointed out there was a type error on the plaque, they agreed. The heading on the replacement plaque reads:

Genevieve Towsley, 1907-1995
Naperville journalist, author and historian

Pamela's poem follows.

Official attention to Genevieve quieted down until she had to have "a bath." Pamela Carpenter and the Corporation were concerned that road salt splashed on her must be removed every year. On the first anniversary we went to Naperville to help Pamela, Bill Smith, and Rita and John give her a mild soap and water bath. Bill has handled it alone since then.

Naperville's 175th anniversary was 2006. Naperville took another good look at its history. The Naperville Herald selected the city's 25 most influential people in its 175 year history. Joseph Naper was number one, of course. Mother was profiled as number 13.

That same year Mother's name was one of those to be placed in the Hall of Honor in the reconstructed Pre-emption House by the Naperville Heritage Society which she helped to found. The lovely ceremony took place during Joe Naper Days in June in Century Chapel, formerly the Episcopal Church which was the society's first project.

In the fall I received a call from Laura Zinger of Channel 17, Naperville's Community Television Station. The station was planning to produce a program about significant Naperville women. Laura was to be the producer of "A Role of Their Own," a documentary about Clarissa Hobson, Hannah Ditzler Alspaugh, Caroline Martin Mitchell, Mattie Eggerman, Genevieve Towsley, Peg Price and Mary Lou Cowlishaw. A one word descriptor is given for each woman as the film is introduced. The word chosen for Mother was "courageous." We went to Naperville for the premier in May, 2007. Older residents attending found themselves a bit confused when they talked with me because it was easy to think they were talking with "Genevieve." Even I think I now look like her.

There continues to be recognitions of and tributes to Genevieve Brayton Towsley for her writing gift to Naperville. This fact is testimony to her significance to this community that loves to admire its past and that it is not just another suburb.

This book from her daughter's perspective is one more of those tributes.

❈ 22 ❈
Friends' and Family Favorites—Genevieve's Recipes

I have mentioned before how Mother was first known for her cooking and baking before she became a noted weekly journalist. She was as much at home with yeast dough as she was with a pen. She was most famous for her caramel pecan rolls. She would give a dozen of this special treat as a Christmas gift, to welcome a neighbor, or as an auction item for a church benefit. I remember one bidder bid over $20 for one dozen rolls; they were that good! Because those close to her knew how special they tasted, we had copies of the recipe available at the reception following her memorial service. There were many other "Towsley Tastes" that still give us special memories. I asked family members for their favorites before starting this last chapter. Their selections are on the following pages.

Making Pecan Rolls

As one way to advertise the book, "A View of Historic Naperville," in October 1975, *The Naperville Sun* featured this recipe in the "Culinary Collectibles" column.

Genevieve's Rolls

Filling (Goo):
8 tablespoons (1/2 cup) butter
2 tablespoons cream
2 tablespoons Karo (dark)
2 cups dark brown sugar
Whole Pecans

Melt butter and add remaining ingredients in order listed, and blend. Do not cook. Makes enough for approximately two dozen rolls—filling and bottom of pans.

Rolls:
1 1/2 cups scalded milk, cooled
½ cup sugar
1 teaspoon salt
3 eggs, beaten
1 package dry yeast softened in ¼ cup water with 2 teaspoons sugar
5 to 5 1/2 cups flour
1 cup butter, melted

In large bowl mix sugar, salt, cooled milk, and softened yeast with one-half of the flour. Add melted butter, and mix in remainder of flour until dough is no longer sticky.

Let dough rise about one hour before putting in refrigerator where it will rise until doubled in bulk. Punch down. Pat salad oil on top of dough while in refrigerator. Dough may be left in refrigerator overnight. For Pecan Rolls, remove one half of dough and let rise in warm room.

Generously grease muffin pans. Place scant teaspoon of "goo" in muffin pans. Top with one whole pecan in each space.

Roll out dough on floured board into rectangle about ¼ inch thick. Spread with "goo" (filling) and sprinkle with cinnamon. Roll up jelly roll fashion and slice about 1 inch thick. Place in pans cut side down. Let rise until double. Bake in 350 degree oven about 20 minutes. Let pan cool about five minutes, then turn out on to cake rack to cool further. Use remainder of refrigerated dough within four days for butter horns or parker house rolls.

Caryl's note: *I have found that the pans must be very well greased. The new silicone baking pans allow the baked rolls to come out of the pan easier. I'm always tempted to put more than a scant teaspoon of goo in each muffin cup. If I do, the rolls stick to the pan. Mother usually substituted half and half for the cream. This recipe makes about 2 dozen rolls.*

This is the doughnut recipe Genevieve used to make the doughnuts she served to the women from Little Friends School when they first came to tell her about their unique project. It was for children whose needs were not being met by the school district. Dottie Krejci remembered the occasion at the memorial service.

Ice Box Doughnuts

3 1/2 cups flour
2 teaspoons baking powder
1 teaspoon soda
½ teaspoon salt
2 eggs
1 cup sugar
I cup sour milk
1 teaspoon vanilla
½ teaspoon nutmeg
3 tablespoons melted butter

Sift and set aside dry ingredients.
Beat eggs, sugar, sour milk together thoroughly.
Stir in dry ingredients, blend well.
Add flavorings and melted butter and stir mixture
    together for 40 strokes
Refrigerate one hour or as much as two or three days.
Roll portion of dough out on floured board to ¼ inch thick.
Cut out doughnuts with doughnut cutter.
Fry in hot fat, turning several times until desired shade of brownness.
May be stored in freezer.
Reheat to serve.

Caryl's note: *The original recipe preceded commercial sour milk (buttermilk). She would substitute with buttermilk in her later years. To reheat a few doughnuts she would put a couple of tablespoons of water in a metal bun warmer, set the doughnuts on a small rack in the warmer, and set on a very low burner. They tasted like fresh doughnuts.*

Mother received this recipe from Alma Effner, whose husband, Lloyd, worked for Illinois Bell Telephone.

Buttermilk Waffles

2 cups flour
1 teaspoon soda
1 teaspoon baking powder
1 teaspoon salt
1 1/2 cups sour or buttermilk
2 eggs
3 tablespoons vegetable oil

> Sift dry ingredients.
> Separate eggs.
> Combine egg yolks, oil and sour milk.
> Stir the liquid into the dry ingredients until smooth.
> Fold in stiffly beaten egg whites.
> Bake on hot waffle irons.

Caryl's note: This was the recipe Marian and I used for the 4H demonstration that we took to the Illinois State Fair. We made waffles a couple times a week for six months practicing so that we would be the county fair winners. That morning at State Fair we were surprised when we went to separate the two eggs. They each had two yolks.

Egg and Ham Brunch Strata

7 slices bread, cubed
1 pound smoked ham, cubed
½ pound sharp cheddar cheese, cubed
3 eggs beaten
2 cups milk
½ teaspoon salt
½ teaspoon dry mustard
¼ pound butter, melted

Mix bread and ham together.
Place in flat 9 x 12 inch flat casserole or pan.
Sprinkle cheese over top.
Beat eggs, milk, mustard and salt and pour over bread and ham and cheese mixture.
Cube 2 slices bread into very small cubes, sprinkle over top.
Pour melted butter over all.
Cover, refrigerate over night.
Bake one hour at 325 degrees.

Serves 8

French Puffs

1 cup hot water
3 tablespoons butter
¼ teaspoon salt
1 cup sifted flour
3 large eggs
Oil or fat for frying

Bring water and butter to a boil.

Add flour all at once. Stir vigorously over medium flame until mixture becomes solid, leaving edges of pan.

Cool slightly. Add one egg at a time, beating one minute after each addition.

Chill one hour or longer in refrigerator.

Heat vegetable oil to 375 or 400 degrees.

Drop mixture from teaspoon (using another to scrape it into hot oil.)

Puffs will usually turn themselves as they brown. Do not remove too soon.

Drain on rack or paper.

While warm, frost with mixture of powdered sugar, cream and vanilla.

Yield—about 40 puffs

Caryl's note: *At the bottom of the recipe card Mother has written: "Gladyce Hemsted recipe." Gladyce was a good friend who gave unique parties. On a day that I forgot to take my lunch to school, Mother brought it to the high school. I found four warm French puffs tucked into the brown bag along with the sandwich. That was a memorable lunch.*

New England Clam Chowder

¼ cup cut-up bacon
1 medium onion ½ cup, chopped
2 cans (6½ ounces each) minced or whole clams
1 medium potato, finely chopped (1 cup)
½ teaspoon salt
dash of pepper
2 cups milk

Cook bacon and onion in 2-quart sauce pan over medium heat, stirring occasionally, until bacon is crisp and onion is tender.

Drain clams, reserving liquor. Add enough water, if necessary, to clam liquor to measure 1 cup

Stir clams, clam liquor, potato, salt and pepper into bacon and onion. Heat to boiling; reduce heat to low, Cover and simmer about 15 minutes or until potato is tender.

Stir in milk. Heat, stirring occasionally, just until hot (do not boil).

Makes about four 1 cup servings.

Caryl's note: *This is what Mother would often fix for us for Saturday lunch. Her recipe with the same amounts of ingredients had quite sketchy directions. This one is from Betty Crocker's New Cook Book.*

It seemed as Dad aged, he became more expressive with his appreciation for Mother's cooking. "This is the best soup I've ever eaten!" he declared one day as he finished a bowl of this chowder.

Mimi's Ham Loaf Balls

1 1/4 pounds ground ham
1 pound ground pork
2 beaten eggs
2 cups soft bread cubes
1 cup milk
1 teaspoon salt

>Combine all ingredients listed.
>Shape into egg shaped balls.
>Place in a 9"x13" pan.

Sauce

½ cup vinegar
½ cup water
1 1/2 cups brown sugar
1 teaspoon dry mustard
10-12 whole cloves

>Combine all above sauce ingredients and bring to a full boil.
>Pour over meat balls.
>Bake in 350 degree oven for 1½ hours.
>After ¾ hour turn balls over-only once.
>Meat balls should be a caramel color.
>If not, bake a little longer.

>Caryl's note: *Our sons called Mother "Mimi." She named the recipe Mimi's Ham Loaf Balls.*

Beer Braten

4 pounds boneless rolled rump beef roast
salt and pepper
1 12 ounce can of beer (or 1 cup vinegar)
4 bay leaves
6 peppercorns
6 whole cloves

Sprinkle meat with salt and pepper.
Place in earthenware bowl only slightly larger than the roast.
Add beer and enough water to cover.
Add bay leaves, peppercorns and cloves.
Cover and let stand in refrigerator for three days, turning night and morning.
Drain meat, saving marinade.
Place in Dutch oven or heavy kettle and brown on all sides.
Meanwhile boil up marinade, until blood coagulates.
Strain marinade through cheese cloth.
Add two cups of strained marinade to meat.
Simmer for 3 hours or until tender.
Remove meat when tender and set aside, keeping warm under foil.

When meat is nearly done, cook desired quantity of noodles.
Brown bread crumbs in butter, set aside.

Gravy

Several rounded tablespoons flour
1 Tablespoon sugar
¼ teaspoon ginger
water

Whisk together vigorously until there are no lumps.
Pour slowly into drippings stirring constantly to desired consistency.

Spoon a serving of noodles, then a serving of beer braten, then the ginger gravy. Top with buttered crumbs on each plate. Or pass each item for guests to serve themselves.

Caryl's notes: *Of all of her recipes this one was probably Dick's favorite. She knew this and when we lived in Chicago, if she hoped we would come to Naperville for the weekend or at least Sunday dinner, she would entice us with her promise to prepare this. It was not included in the first set of recipes she gave me because she wanted it to be something special only she did for Dick. Only after they moved to the retirement center did she share it.*

Sweet Potato Casserole

5 pounds fresh sweet potatoes

16 ounces (1 jar) orange marmalade

¼ pound butter, melted

salt to taste

large marshmallows, cut in half crosswise-enough to cover top of baking dish

    Cook sweet potatoes till tender.
    Peel while warm.
    Mash with mixer.
    Mix in melted butter and marmalade.
    Salt to taste.
    Put mixture in greased casserole.
    Bake at 350 degrees until heated through.
    Top with marshmallow halves.
    Put back in oven until marshmallows are toasted.
    Watch with care (5-10 minutes) to prevent burning.

    Caryl's note: *This recipe was a Thanksgiving favorite.*

Genevieve's Pumpkin Pie

2 eggs
1 cup canned pumpkin
½ teaspoon ground cinnamon
½ teaspoon ground ginger
¼ teaspoon ground cloves
¼ teaspoon ground nutmeg
½ teaspoon salt
½ cup sugar
2 tablespoons dark New Orleans molasses
2 scant cups milk, heated to luke warm
1 unbaked pie shell, pricked with a fork.

    Beat two eggs in mixing bowl.
    Place 1 cup of pumpkin in blob on top of eggs.
    Do not blend yet!
    Put spices and salt in depression in pumpkin.
    Mix into pumpkin and blend into eggs.
    Add ½ cup sugar, the molasses and luke warm milk.
    Blend well and pour into unbaked pie shell.
    Bake in 400 degree oven for 15 minutes.
    Turn heat down to 325 degrees.
    Bake until silver knife inserted comes out clean.
    Serve with whipped topping.
    Enjoy!

    Caryl's note: *We did enjoy! This pumpkin pie is so much more flavorful than any others I've tasted. If given a choice, I never choose a pumpkin pie for dessert unless I can be sure it was made with her recipe. Mother believed it was the dark molasses that gave it that special flavor.*

Lemon Fluff

<u>Crust</u>

¼ pound very cold butter
1 cup flour
1 tablespoon sugar

Mix together with hands and pat dough to form a crust in 9 inch square pan. Bake in moderate oven until light brown. Cool.

<u>Filling</u>

1 Tablespoon Knox gelatine dissolved in 2 tablespoons cold water.
4 egg yolks
½ cup sugar
Juice and rind of 1 lemon
¼ teaspoon salt

Cook last five ingredients in double boiler.
Add gelatine and let COOL.
Beat 4 egg whites stiff and add ½ cup sugar.
Fold egg custard that has started to congeal into beaten whites.
Place in cold crust and refrigerate several hours.
Serve with whipped cream.

(Serves 8)

Grace Fredenhagen's recipe

Caryl's note: *This was her favorite "elegant" dessert for bridge club or special parties. The buttery crust complemented the creamy lemon filling so nicely. I always hoped there would be a leftover slice or two.*

Christmas Crescents

½ pound butter
½ cup sugar
1 teaspoon vanilla
¼ pound almonds, ground
2 cups flour

>Mix together well.
>Form crescent shaped cookies with your hands.
>Place on flat cookie sheet ¾ inch apart.
>Chill in refrigerator for 15 minutes.
>Bake in 32 5-350 degree oven until PALE brown-approximately 8-10 minutes.
>Don't get too brown!
>Roll in powdered sugar when cool
>Store in tight can.

(Aunt Mae Foucek's recipe)

Caryl's note: Aunt Mae was the aunt of a friend of hers. This was my favorite Christmas cookie of all that she made. There never were any crescents left over any time they were served. It is important to make this recipe with "real" butter. No butter substitute can provide that special flavor that real dairy butter does. I've tried it and been disappointed.

As I've read through each of these recipes, copied them and remembered her preparing them, I marvel how she managed to write so prolifically and cook so creatively. She was highly proficient in both skills.

Printed in the United States
204592BV00001B/256-273/P